The
RESURRECTION

The Unopened Gift

Gerard Chrispin

The Resurrection
The Unopened Gift

With heartfelt thanks to God for the vibrant example
and constant encouragement of Professor Verna
Wright who always helped me 'on to victory.'

Contents

Author, Broadcaster, and Pastor/Teacher of Grace Community Church, Sun Valley, California

The resurrection of Christ is the very essence of what Christianity is all about. It is the culmination and the nucleus of the gospel message. It embodies our hopes for triumph over sin and death, and at the same time it proves that Christ has already won that triumph.

The resurrection also reminds us that we serve a risen, living Lord. He Himself is the resurrection and the life and the very personification of eternal life itself. 'He is not the God of the dead, but the God of the living' (cf. Mark 12 verse 27). Life, resurrection life, infuses every facet of the Christian faith.

The resurrection is the ground of our assurance, it is the basis for all our future hopes, and it is the source of power in our daily lives here and now. It gives us courage in the midst of persecution, comfort in the midst of trials, and hope in the midst of this world's darkness.

The church needs to recover the truth of the resurrection. We lose focus too easily. We get bogged down in the trials of this life. We become absorbed in mundane things. And we forget the power Christ's resurrection has to elevate us above all that. We constantly need to have our attention brought back to what really matters. And nothing matters more to a Christian than the resurrection of our Lord.

That's why I'm thankful for Gerard Chrispin's book 'The Resurrection: the unopened gift.' He unwraps the meaning and the power of the resurrection and sets it forth in clear and compelling style. He shows why we believe Christ is risen. He explains the rich meaning and implications of the resurrection in our lives. The book is appropriate either as an introduction to Christianity for the seeking heart, or as a helpful handbook for believers. Wherever you are in your spiritual journey, the book you hold in your hands will give you a fresh and invigorating perspective on the resurrection of Christ.

My prayer is that the book will find a wide audience among believers and unbelievers alike. May it kindle a flame of hope and faith that nothing can extinguish.

John MacArthur,
Sun Valley, California, USA

Author's preface

It is a privilege to write a book which focuses on the resurrection of the Lord Jesus Christ. I am grateful to Jim Holmes of Great Writing and to Digby James of Quinta Press for their help in getting this edition in print via 119Press and Amazon. I am also grateful to John MacArthur for his encouraging words in his preface, and to Stephen Wright for his comments on the back cover.

Like Jesus Himself and like the gospel message centred on Him, the resurrection is staggeringly miraculous yet provably and historically factual. It is objectively true yet subjectively experienced by all who trust and follow Christ. We never know who the next person will be who will be transformed through the risen Lord. Yet we see time and again the parallel way that very different lives are so totally changed because of Christ's death and resurrection. That is why Jesus said it was like being 'born again.'

The resurrection's historicity and meaning are fully endorsed by the Bible, God's word, and thus needs no human approval, but it is acknowledged to be historically true even without reference to the authority of God's word. Examining Christ's resurrection is academically satisfying to the most learned of people and yet its effects and meaning are understood by many with little education. Jesus' rising from the tomb is absolutely vital to the very existence of real Christianity yet ridiculed and attacked by many people including some who are very religious but who have never received the risen Christ in their hearts and lives. It is timeless in its applications: it is never out of date. It guarantees an everlasting and blessed future in Heaven and yet gives eternal life now on earth.

The resurrection could not save any man or woman unless Jesus had first borne on the cross that person's sin and punishment due: but if the cross had been the end and Jesus had not risen from the dead then no-one could ever have been forgiven and saved. That is why the apostle Paul emphasised these vital twin truths together when he said,

'I delivered to you first of all that which I also received: that Christ died for our sins according to the Scriptures, and that He was buried, and that He rose again the third day according to the Scriptures' (1 Corinthians 15:3–4)

Committed Christians are indwellt by the risen Christ through the Holy Spirit. Thus we are always helped, blessed, comforted and encouraged as we seek to get to know our risen Saviour and Lord better. This is done on a daily basis by reading the Bible and praying personally. We are greatly helped each week by spending time meeting together on Sundays in our churches for worship and fellowship with others who have also come to know the power of Jesus' resurrection in daily living. Each Sunday we remind ourselves that Jesus rose on the first day of the week by calling it the 'Lord's Day.' During the week we also enjoy Bible studies and prayer times together.

My prayer is that this book will help us all to get closer to the risen Lord of glory. May it encourage us all to unpack and benefit from God's amazing gift of blessings that are ours through the Lord Jesus' resurrection. May this gift of His grace not go unopened! There is much blessing ahead!

Gerard A. Chrispin

Introduction

'Oh, not that again!' I thought, as I drove towards the M3 motorway from Southampton to London. It was Easter time, heralded by the brightness of the yellow daffodils on the large traffic island I had just passed.

The first item on the BBC news concerned another denial by a prominent church leader of the resurrection of the Lord Jesus Christ. My mind worked overtime. I wondered what effect remarks like these might have on those who had never seriously considered the Christian message. Would fledgling Christians see the difference the remarks showed between being 'religious' and belonging to Christ? How would Bible believing Christians in the same church as this eminent sceptic react?

I hardly noticed that I had already entered the motorway. I had been lost in thought. The previous time I had heard the resurrection under serious attack was when I discussed it with some convinced Muslim friends. I had seriously and constructively debated with them the evidence for the resurrection of Jesus, and left them a copy of Josh McDowell's book, *The Islam Debate*.

The BBC announcement revealed that the 'reverend gentleman' shared their views that Christ had not risen bodily from the dead and that He was less than the eternal Son of God and the all-powerful God the Son.

I admired the sincerity of my Muslim friends. True, I was very concerned at their misunderstanding of history and of the Bible but I had not expected them to agree with me on these issues. One would have been surprised if they had afforded to the Lord Jesus Christ what the hymn states is the 'highest name that Heaven affords'. On the other hand, I felt sure that these lines must have been sung many times by the ecclesiastical critic from Christian England. How sad that he could so blatantly deny the very teaching he was employed—and paid—to teach!

My mind went back to a previous Easter. A committed Christian gentleman had paid for the Easter message 'He is risen!' to be franked by the Post Office on to thousands of envelopes despatched throughout Britain. What a furore that had caused! Whilst multitudes of Christians from many different churches and denominations rejoiced in the timely reminder of the good news, others complained bitterly. Freedom of the press, it seemed, should not be extended to a sincere man's desire to remind a materialistic society of the central truth of historic Christianity at Easter. Why, I thought, was there opposition to sharing resurrection truth? What would be the effect of attacking one of the twin truths of Christianity? Would it have really mattered if Jesus Christ had not risen from the tomb?

Can any good come from the controversy?

There are some positive results from this combined opposition of other religions, modernist churchianity, optimistic humanism, and growing occult forces (some appearing as wolves in sheep's clothing, as in the so- called New Age Movement). At least the battleground has been chosen! And the informed Christian would prefer to maintain his cause in no better arena than that of whether Jesus Christ rose from the dead. Explaining why God loves rebels like ourselves would be harder. It would be harder still to find reasons for his persistent, generous mercy and help when we fail Him so often. But to defend the resurrection! That was like 'playing at home!'

It is good to know that our trust in the risen Saviour has a foundation of objective truth. It is also, however, a subjective experience. The scientist demanded facts. The existentialist asked for experience. The Christian always has had, does have, and will have both: Christ crucified and risen again may dwell in our hearts by faith!

So the challenge to foundational Christian beliefs has strengthened many Christians in their faith. In the case of this book it was the challenge from the opposers of the traditional and still relevant Gospel, plus the desire of young Christians at meetings of Young Life to hear the answer from the Bible and history, that caused it to be written.

You will have gathered by now that I welcome serious investigation into the resurrection because it emphasises that Christianity is rooted in fact and history. He really IS risen! His death on the cross for my sins is effective to save me, and His resurrection life underlines it!

Yet I have encountered an ignorance even amongst evangelical churches of various denominations concerning the significance of the resurrection in every day living and in Christian belief. Was the resurrection just a 'macro miracle' to show we had got something that other religions did not have? The church, in common with the world, has an unhealthy craving for 'signs and wonders.' Is the resurrection just an older and bigger manifestation of the dramatic and spine tingling experiences which monopolise some bookstalls today?

Or are there life-changing truths to be learned from and applied with the resurrection?

As I drew nearer to London that Easter time, I wondered as I still do, what answers we would get if a one question questionnaire was distributed for response to all our churches, Christian Unions, Young Life Branches, Bible Colleges, and Missionary Societies. The question? 'How is your daily living affected by the resurrection of the Lord Jesus Christ and why?'

Do we know why it is important that Christ rose again from the dead?

This book is essentially in two parts. The first is chapter one which works through the evidence for the bodily resurrection of the Lord Jesus Christ. Some Christians may be unsure. This chapter shows that Christianity is not built on a myth, but on a miracle. Part two is the rest of the book. Some may say, 'Jesus rose from the grave. So what?' If you do not think it, that attitude may still secretly determine how you live the Christian life. This is why I have written the other chapters of the book. The resurrection of Jesus had purposes behind it. Those purposes are very down to earth for all of us, whether we are believers or unbelievers.

The resurrection is a key teaching. This key opens up the door to lead us to real blessing. May the resurrection key open up the truth of God's word to you. The biggest blessing will always come when you read the Bible, with an open heart, to concentrate on its simple, infallible and divine teaching, and then to do what it says.

From time to time we hear of people who have won a valuable prize and never gone to collect it. There was even a lottery winner who could not be traced! Whilst I would never buy a lottery ticket under any circumstances, and appreciate the problems that suddenly gained huge wealth can bring to a selfish human heart, I could empathise a little with someone who was probably living very modestly when untold riches were his (or hers) but of no value simply because they were not claimed! The blessings that have their source in the resurrection and that can flow to the mind, heart and will of the person yielding to and walking with the risen Lord are immense. But so often they are like an unopened gift. They are there to be appropriated. No 'magic' words or dramatic experience is needed to claim that prize. Simply an understanding of the truth that sets us free and a yielding to that truth, by God's grace and help, will make the poorest of us see how rich we are and can be in our Saviour who conquered death. To change the illustration, imagine that a gift of great value and usefulness is kept wrapped up, rather than being opened, appropriated and enjoyed. What a waste! How stupid! Yet the resurrection of the Lord Jesus Christ is like that immensely valuable and uniquely useful gift. So often we look at it, but do not enjoy it or benefit from it. I hope that, under God, this book will help us to do just that regarding Jesus Christ's resurrection.

One final point. The aspects of the resurrection are so inevitably interwoven and interlinked that each chapter covers some ground that will already be familiar. This is not mere repetition; it will be the same scenery from a different viewpoint, the background context essentially the same, but the angle of observation changing as we move through the book. The conclusion of each chapter will be the same! The answer is in the crucified and risen Lord of glory!

Thus, although the book stands as a whole, the resurrection, and the Gospel, should be clearly understandable from each chapter. May those looking for fresh reality, those newly converted and dedicated disciples find real spiritual food and blessing, under God's grace, from each chapter of this book. I also pray that some may come to know the risen Saviour, whilst others who have wandered far off may come back to the living and loving Shepherd of the sheep.

The resurrection: did it really happen?

Was it delusion, fraud, swoon, mistake or miracle?

Start at the beginning

D id the resurrection of Jesus Christ really happen? Many authors have clearly shown the strength of the evidence for the resurrection of Jesus Christ from the dead. Their number has included professors, historians, archeologists, doctors and practising lawyers. Unlike many religions, which melt under the searching light of deep investigation, Biblical Christianity thrives under probing examination. The reason? He IS risen!

So if I did not set out primarily to prove the resurrection, why begin with the evidences?

My answer is simple. It is good to grasp the significance of the truths which are built on the resurrection, but unless we realize that these 'truths' really are true we cannot build our lives on them. Many claims are based on subjective experience alone and are never able to be substantiated. But an experience that is based on solid fact is not only individually real, but can be objectively investigated. In short, you can test the claim.

This first chapter is thus intended to be a bridge between the evidence that Christ conquered death, and a personal consideration of what that can mean in your life.

A former Lord Chief Justice claimed that the resurrection of Jesus Christ was one of the best attested facts in ancient history. Was he right? Is it true, as an eminent Professor of Law observed, that there is more evidence for the resurrection of Jesus than for the existence of Julius Caesar? If so, why?

The need to make up your mind

You are like a jury. Your thoughts, logical processes, deductions, feelings, and inclinations are to be used to reach a calculated, decisive judgment.

Neutrality is not an option. Either Jesus rose and rightly demands your attention, repentance, trust and obedience, or He stayed dead. If He only became a rotting corpse why should you follow Him?

How should the jurors behave? Personal preferences and prejudices must be kept carefully in check. They will want to speak loudly at times! Tell them to be objective and fair—and not simply to repeat what others have said.

In his book, *Man Alive*, Michael Green warns about two obstructive forms of prejudice. One argues as follows: 'I do not believe that the resurrection is possible as dead men do not come back from the grave. Thus Jesus could not have done so either!' The other wears a pseudo-theological garb and states 'My theological or philosophical position is unaffected by the resurrection, so I do not need to believe Jesus was resurrected bodily— therefore I do not believe He rose again!'

The purpose in examining the resurrection is to ascertain if He really did rise again. If so, we have found an exception to the generally observed rule that the dead don't rise. Similarly, if it can be shown that He did conquer death, it is high time certain theologians re-theologized and certain philosophers looked more carefully into their ideas to check if they are correct.

Common ground

There is an amazing accord between nearly all the friends and foes of Christianity, about the historical facts surrounding the life and death of Christ. This is probably because of all well-known celebrities, Christ's life is the most closely attested by reliable eye-witnesses. The fact that He died and three days later the tomb was empty is what the lawyer calls common ground. Nearly all thinking people accept that there was an empty tomb. Some would read different implications into this, while others on principle or just to be pig-headed, declare themselves to disbelieve it. They would never apply the same rule to any other great event of history, even if the evidence for it from writings of the day was infinitely weaker.

Interestingly, one rarely meets a genuine historian who doubts the empty tomb. The overwhelming manuscript evidence is too persuasive, both Biblical, and extra-Biblical sources provided by Josephus (AD 70), Tacitus (AD 100), and Pliny (AD 95). Professor F. F. Bruce and Prof. Ken Kitchen have also both shown that we must not sell short the accuracy of the Bible records. Time and again accounts in both the Old and New Testaments have been vindicated by the archeologist. We can also apply an internal audit to the New Testament. The facts it relates never contradict themselves, nor those found in the Old Testament. Its record is staggering! And it points clearly to the empty tomb.

What is this common ground, generally held by honest men, whether Christian or not?

1. Jesus Christ lived. Even the coin in your pocket testifies to the birth of One who split time into 'BC' ('before Christ') and 'AD' ('The year of the Lord' or, if you prefer, 'after Christ').

2. He was crucified between two criminals in the packed-out city of Jerusalem. The complete event was so dramatic, climactic, and supernatural as to be unforgettable by all who witnessed it. Many of those witnesses later claimed to have met the risen Christ.

3. He was laid in another man's tomb, and the third day the tomb was empty.

4. Neither friend nor foe, disciple nor disbeliever, ever produced the dead body.

5. Many claimed they had met the risen Christ. Some paid for that testimony with their own lives. No-one who met Jesus after the resurrection found Him to be exactly the same, in a physical sense, as He had been before the crucifixion. Also no-one claimed to meet Him again after Saul of Tarsus' startling encounter on the Damascus road.

Strange, you might think, if Jesus had not risen that someone somewhere did not find the missing link. Yes—a decaying body; a depressed or fraudulent carpenter trying to avoid the public gaze and scorn; or the re- emergence of the 'miracle man' somewhere else. But the line went dead! If Jesus did not rise from the dead, what did happen? Where did He go? With whom did He associate? Why did He stay hidden? How could He do it? Why do it anyhow?

More questions are raised by a failed resurrection than are answered by a factual one!

But some have sought to explain it away—even accepting the 'common ground,' and we will examine their hypotheses in brief, now.

Was it simply delusion?

The delusion theory is that those who claimed to have met the risen Christ were mistaken, albeit sincerely. They were victims of hallucination, or some other trick of the mind and memory, because of their unstable emotional state. It is easy to repeat this view, but is it really valid?

Why not question your family doctor, next time you see him? Ask him whether he has ever heard of an identical delusion affecting hundreds of different people, of different temperaments, ages and backgrounds, in different places, at different times, and in different circumstances! Find out if it is a normal occurrence! Insist that you are not looking merely at similar symptoms that you might find in the excitement of a big crowd, but at identical experiences whether in large numbers or in ones and twos. Then ask him, on the far out chance that this were hypothetically possible, would it be expected that every person claiming this experience should find that their delusions or hallucinations stopped at the same point in time, seven weeks after the claimed resurrection! Would not some of them, at least, find their illness carrying on longer than others?

After the Doctor, visit the nearest lawyer. Does he think the evidence of hundreds of independent eye witnesses is weak or strong—especially when it never conflicts. Five hundred people claiming to have met the risen Lord Jesus Christ in those few weeks, often in broad daylight, would delight the heart of any advocate presenting evidence in court. Can you see the witnesses waiting to be called? The benches outside the court are filled with those who say they met Him on the very day of His resurrection: Mary Magdalene, the women who had prepared the tomb beforehand, Peter, the two travellers on the Emmaus Road, and all the apostles except Thomas.

Others who saw Him later wait their turn to enter the witness box. Even good old 'doubting Thomas' is there to say he didn't believe it until he too met Him face to face. Seven who saw Him by Lake Tiberias endorse the evidence of the five hundred who, with the apostles, encountered Him on the mountain. James and the eleven also add that He was with them at Jerusalem and Bethany. Amazing delusion! No wonder that when He appeared in a unique way to Saul of Tarsus (later called the Apostle Paul) on the Damascus Road, in a brightness that outshone the mid-day sun, Saul, readily accepted His claim to be the resurrected Lord Jesus. He had heard and fought against the evidence. Now he honestly faced the fact that this was truth about the One Who is truth!

Many of these same witnesses were then persecuted by a hostile world, sealing their testimony with their blood, rather than deny the undeniable. The witnesses were of the highest calibre.

Was it a case of fraud?

Fraud is a crime. Every lover of Agatha Christie stories knows the two *whodunit* questions. First, who could have done it? Second, who would have done it? Opportunity and motive! Who had the ability and the chance? Who had the motivation and the desire? Whoever fits both criteria is a suspect for closer questioning.

Before looking at the theory that the body of Jesus was stolen, an important point needs to be made. Normally the criminal who had been crucified would have been thrown on the ever burning rubbish dump, Gehenna, outside Jerusalem. The same word is used in the Bible to describe hell, the place of everlasting conscious torment separate from God's loving presence. A criminal's corpse was despised and certainly did not 'merit' burial. Thus it could have been possible, though difficult, to secretly steal the mutilated body. However it would have been impossible to dress it up as a gloriously resurrected body! Pilate was thus happy to grant the request of Joseph of Arimathea to give Jesus a decent burial in his tomb. It meant less problems for the authorities as it would clearly be more difficult to steal the body from a sealed tomb than from a rubbish tip. Unsuccessful in burning the body, the Jewish leaders secure a guard for the tomb, thinking they can now rest in peace!

We should not relegate the prospect of His glorious resurrection to the realm of the escape artist, but remember that Houdini made escape as difficult as possible before he broke free. The enemies of Jesus had only to keep that body dead for three days. They tried to make it impossible for it to be stolen. Houdini was not dead when he started his skilful escape act. The Lord Jesus Christ was dead and His body was embalmed and cocooned in tightly wrapped bandages. Either someone broke into the grave, removed the body without disturbing the grave clothes, and broke out again leaving the stone sealing the entry and the guard blissfully unaware, or the Lord Himself broke free from the chains of death. Either way, Houdini is relegated to the bottom of the fourth division in comparison!

But we are running ahead of ourselves. We must objectively consider whether someone dishonestly snatched the body from the tomb of Joseph of Arimathea? Did an ingenious third party fake the resurrection? If so, who had both opportunity and motive? And could the person, or persons, carry out their crime successfully, without detection then or later?

Imagine the scene. A beaten and flogged Jesus has been crucified. After being speared by a professional soldier to make sure He was dead, He has been tightly wrapped in suffocating and constricting bandages. He is taken to a tomb. One hundred pounds weight of spices are put on that battered, bruised, torn and lifeless body. A heavy sealing stone is securely rolled in front of the tomb, and soldiers are put on duty outside to deal with whoever may come to rob the tomb. Note that they check the security of the tomb first. No doubt professionalism ensured that they checked the contents as well. They then had the tomb sealed with a large stone—just in case.

Who could those potential thieves be? The disciples? The Scribes, Pharisees, or priests? May be some of the soldiers themselves? Or perhaps someone else— who can tell what weird things some people get up to!

Let us ask again: who could steal the body, who would do it, and who would be successful? It is obvious that the body had to be removed and disposed of if a false claim that Jesus had risen from the dead was to be made. Why? Because you cannot have a fraud masquerading as a risen Redeemer if someone could quietly take him by the hand and show him the corpse still in the tomb. The resurrection, indeed, could have attracted Sherlock Holmes too in The Case of the Missing Corpse! For fraud to occur, the body must disappear! But who would steal it?

Were the disciples the thieves?

Could the disciples have snatched the corpse? Certainly not! They were frightened, scattered and hiding! They had shrunk from being identified with their Master when He was with them. Would they be braver without Him than with Him? In any case, would they have even attempted to overpower the soldiers? And could they have succeeded not only in overcoming the soldiers but in doing it so quietly that they could hoodwink others into believing that the resurrection had happened? Remember that their Teacher had told them not to lie, not to brawl, and not to cheat. Would they devote the rest of their lives to continuing that teaching by perpetrating a huge fraud after having beaten up or cheated men lawfully protecting the tomb!

The story, put out by the leaders of the Jews as a smoke-screen around the resurrection, was that the disciples came and stole the body.[1] This fabricated rumour was achieved by the soldiers having been bribed by the Jewish leaders. They were assured of protection if the matter came to the Governor's ears. The soldiers were to say that whilst they were asleep the disciples stole the body! Many a lawyer would like to have the captain of the guards in court to ask how he, or his men, knew that the disciples had stolen the body if they were asleep when the grave-robbers came! Perhaps it was a night-cap of Horlicks that allowed such deep sleep that they were not woken up by the breaking in and rolling away of the large sealed stone!

An interesting fact is that there is no record of their having been disciplined in any way for what would have been an inexcusable breach of duty and discipline. This is strong evidence that their superiors knew the story was false. It is very unlikely that the rumour would have gone by without being heard and examined by them. This is further evidence that they were not asleep on the job. If, however, the risen Lord had passed through the tomb in His resurrection body, He would not have been visible unless He chose to appear to them.

But how did the soldiers know who stole the body if they were all asleep? How did the disciples move the huge stone without waking them? Were all the professionals asleep at the same time when they had been given the military task of guarding the tomb? Why waste time removing the body from the covering graveclothes when they got inside the tomb? Would they not rather cut and run? Then where did they hide the body, and how did they then stage the resurrection appearances? Why on earth did some of them then lay down their lives, claiming loyalty to their risen Saviour before life itself? Many weighty questions! No solid answers!

Some have made the superficial accusation that the disciples bribed the soldiers! But here were men of small means. Would the guard be bought off lightly, if at all, when the death sentence for neglect of duty could face them? And, again, this would deny the changed character and courage of the men who later turned the world upside down with their sincere message of a crucified and risen Lord. Further, the problem remains of staging the resurrection appearances convincingly.

Do the disciples strike you as a swashbuckling unprincipled band of opportunist cheats with no love or concern for their Saviour and His teachings? At the crucifixion do they strike you as brimming with confidence and on the brink of success, or as a stunned, depressed, cowering and defeated collection of frightened and disillusioned men? After meeting the Victor of the resurrection are you struck most by their fraudulent behaviour or their new found boldness, by their self-seeking scheming or by their devouring passion to present Christ to sinful and dying men and women? You be the judge. What interest could they possibly have had in both living and dying for a lie they knew they had made themselves?

Did the leaders of the Jews steal the body?

The Jewish leaders could not have taken the body either. Contact with a dead body would not only have made them unclean, but would have broken their Sabbath rules. Everyone would wonder what they were doing if they were seen out. And what was their motive? They had wanted Jesus on the cross, and the body on the fire. Even the second best of the tomb need only last for three days to prove the Carpenter a fraud. They needed that body in that tomb. They had requested the guard. They had paid the soldiers guarding it to keep it safe because of the unfounded fear that the disciples would come to steal it, and the rules of their ceremonial uncleanness prevented them doing the unsavoury task themselves.

But assume, for a minute, that logic and circumstances are turned upside-down and that somehow the Jewish leaders took the body. Do you need a degree in logic to know how to bury the resurrection once and for all? Produce the body, and watch the damp squib of Christianity fizzle out before it even gets going.

It is a key fact, and an irresistible argument against all theories denying the resurrection of Jesus, that no-one at any time in any place ever produced the body or the remains of our Lord. That would have settled it!

Did the guards double cross?

We need not waste too much time on the theory that the guarding soldiers stole the body. No doubt they could have had the opportunity to steal it, if they were of sufficiently low calibre, and if their officers were of the same mind as the fraudulent rank and file. But why do it? The death sentence would almost certainly await them if they were found out. And even if loss of life could have been avoided, would it have been worth losing job and freedom for this motiveless act? How could they keep secret the criminal act they were to prevent? Would not at least one of them have squealed? Surely s link would have broken under the inevitable vigorous interrogation which would have followed?

Above all, what would their motive be? Pleasing the Jews? But the Jews wanted the carpenter's dead son in the tomb. Antagonizing the Jews? This was too risky. Sooner or later truth would escape and they would be extremely vulnerable from both sides as trouble-makers. Perhaps they tried to please the disciples by bolstering them falsely? But why? And in any case how could men of integrity be bolstered by, and in some cases die for, a dishonest trick? No, the suspicion of the guards as the grave robbers would leave us with no motive and even less chance of success.

A final word on fraud

What is true of the disciples, the Jewish leaders and the guards is true for any and all suspects who were under investigation as body snatchers. Where was the opportunity, what was the motive, and how could they avoid detection? The fact is that no-one could have successfully stolen the body and enabled the consequent lie of the resurrection to have been believed. There is not a shred of reasonable evidence to support that possibility. We must also note that if any of the main three groups of suspects had taken the body, they would have had to survive the careful scrutiny of the other two groups, as well as duping over five hundred witnesses.

From time to time someone somewhere will suggest a new culprit. Or an old theory will be resurrected as a 'new fad' for a while. Each one will fail under the criteria discussed above.

Joseph of Arimathea is a more recent favourite. As Jesus was laid in his tomb, we are told, he could have stolen the body. He was not cowering away, it is true. But his profile was all the higher because his tomb was used. He would be under even closer scrutiny. Was he not, in any case, a man of integrity? What would he gain from his deceit, even had he accomplished it? How did he get around the guards? How did he, on his own, fool the huge crowd of eye-witnesses? Again we ask—could he and would he have been able to successfully take the body, secretly dispose of it, and stage the well-witnessed post-resurrection appearances? And why would he want to do so? He had already arranged that Christ should be given a fitting burial. Joseph had honoured the body of the Lord Jesus by the generous gift of his own tomb. Without it the corpse would have been greatly dishonoured by being thrown on to what was effectively a rubbish dump. Bearing in mind the dignity given by Joseph to Christ's body, would he desecrate it by disturbing it after the burial?

Did Jesus merely swoon?

The view that Jesus merely swooned has the doubtful distinction that it unites together modernist theologians (some of whom nevertheless still claim to be Christians!) with fundamentalist Muslims (who follow their religion with more consistency than the former!). Both groups deny the Deity, substitutionary atonement and bodily resurrection of the Lord Jesus Christ. But are they right? Is logic, quite apart from Scripture, on their side?

We are asked to believe that Jesus did not die on the cross. Ironically a large amount of a certain type of 'faith' is necessary to accept that view. But we are told that He merely passed out: He fainted, or swooned. He was taken down from the cross, put in the tomb, revived, escaped without disturbing the sleeping guards, and then (being an unscrupulous fraud Himself) appeared with such composure and in such a glowing state of health that a large cross section of people were convinced that He had risen from the dead.

Full marks for imagination, but in terms of credibility it floats like a lead balloon! Medically, psychologically, morally, and logically it is a theory of straw.

Medical diagnosis of the view

Have you ever seen a television interview with the battered loser of a heavyweight boxing championship just after they have picked him off the floor? Were you impressed with his well-being and composure? Would he convince you that he could now beat anyone?

Jesus had not fought for the heavyweight championship of the world over fifteen rounds and lost! He had been flogged with thirty nine stripes by the cruel three thonged whip. These thongs often had lead and bone attached, resulting in a cruel tearing of the flesh. Men could die from that flogging alone. The soldiers had beaten Him. The Bible says His face was terribly marred. His beard was plucked out, in fulfilment of Isaiah chapter 50 verse 6. His hands and feet were nailed to a cross. Iron had pierced His flesh. He had hung there in agony for six hours of torture with no water to drink. His side had then been pierced by the Roman soldier's spear. He had been pronounced dead by the executioners. His wrecked body was taken down and tightly wrapped in constricting bandages for burial. No medical aid was given. After all, why try to heal a corpse, or alleviate its suffering? He was laid in a cold hard tomb, with nothing to eat and, more importantly, nothing to drink. There were no doctors and nurses. No intensive care. We are asked to believe that having been mistakenly declared dead, after three days in this miserable state Jesus revived, unwrapped the graveclothes, wrapped them up again to make it look as though He had passed through them, quietly rolled a huge sealed stone aside from the inside of the tomb without waking the sleeping guards, and escaped. Having cleaned Himself up,

He recovered so unbelievably well from His wounds and ordeal that He could appear here and there, without announcement or anticipation, so as to convince a large number of people in different circumstances that He was the risen Lord of glory! That story takes much more faith than any Christian has a right to demand of an agnostic!

Need anything else be said on that subject? Perhaps not, except to quote the opinion of the internationally acclaimed physician, Professor Verna Wright. Talking of the blood and water that came from the wound caused by the Centurion's spear, he suggested that this possibly marked the recent separation of the clot from the serum when the pericardial sack was pierced by the spear. Jesus may have died, medically speaking, from cardial tamponade (acute heart failure to the layman).

Note also that the examination of the professional soldier at the execution revealed He was already dead. Normally soldiers would hasten the death of the victims of crucifixion by breaking their legs. This made it virtually impossible for the suspended victim to push up and gasp air into his lungs. He would die by asphyxiation. With Jesus there was no need to break His legs (which incidentally fulfilled Biblical prophecy of the suffering Messiah that none of His bones would be broken). He had already died. The spearing of Jesus by the soldier was not savage vandalism, but simply to make doubly sure what he already knew (incidentally also fulfilling a second prophecy). According to Professor Wright's explanation, the spear could have passed through the rib cage and pierced His heart (pericardial sack). The prophecy of the Passover Lamb having been slain had come to pass.[2]

A fair-minded assessment must reject the swoon theory. It is inconceivable that Jesus merely lost consciousness only to recover and present Himself in such a way as to convince people that He was the Son of God who had risen from the dead.

What would the psychologist make of the swoon theory?

Back to the interview with the battered loser! Covered in massive bruising, with congealing but still weeping wounds, Christ stands, or rather, tries to stand on nail pierced feet. He opens His mouth and says, 'Why are you troubled? And why do doubts arise in your hearts? Look at my hands and my feet.' He says to Thomas, 'Reach your hand here and put it into my side.' The sight before them and the horror of being asked to look at and even touch those unhealed wounds would be all the evidence they needed that He had not risen from death.[3] Would they have been convinced of glorious resurrection by such a battered fraud? They were already depressed, defeated, scared, and in hiding. Could their lives have been so changed by this that they later 'turned the world upside down?'

Remember that they were not expecting or pre-disposed to the resurrection. True they were not all as hard a nut to crack as sceptical Doubting Thomas, but neither were they easy to convince.[4] Note the depressive use of the past tense in the language of the two travellers on the road to Emmaus. They spoke of Jesus who 'had been' a prophet. There was no question of a Jesus as the risen and eternal Son of God in the present tense! That was until Jesus made Himself known to them both from the Scriptures and by opening their eyes to His risen presence.

Surely a mutilated, lacerated, dehydrated, and utterly exhausted victim of such violence—whom the executioners had thought was dead even before He was speared—could never have convinced anyone of His resurrection, even with psychological preparation which, in this case was most definitely non-existent!

Morality says no swoon

The moral inconsistency of Jesus stage managing His own crucifixion (leaving Himself perilously close to dying!) and then foisting a false resurrection on an incredibly gullible world, is ridiculous. This is the One whose moral teaching in the Sermon on the Mount is unsurpassable, as many non-Christians wholeheartedly agree. Here is One whose influence has consistently made bad men good and good men better. No-one can examine His life, His teaching, and His effect on those who knew Him most closely (and consequently His failures if He had any) without echoing with hard-necked Pilate, 'I find no fault in Him.' A comparison of our moral failure and inconsistency with His faultlessness would lead us to confess the enormity of the gulf. Judas, the spy in the camp, would have revealed the moral lapses of Christ, had there been any. Instead, after betraying Jesus, he went out in remorse and shame.

Would the disciples die for a lying fraud? Would their lives be filled with self-sacrifice and loving service to others in support of such a cheat! They lived alongside the resurrected Christ and knew He was really resurrected. Truth became their badge and integrity their compulsive life style, whatever the cost.

Is swoon logical?

Now ignore every argument presented against the swoon theory. Try to assume He did not die and that His resurrection was a remarkable recovery from a faint because of rest and recuperation in the tomb!

Now please answer the following questions. Where did He live afterwards? Where and when did He finally die? Why did no-one hear of Him again? What happened to His popularity, and why? Why did the disciples ignore Him seven weeks after He recovered? Why did He not help them in their work after that? Why did they insist, at pain of imprisonment, persecution, and death, that He had died and had risen from the dead? Take up John's Gospel and read chapter 19 verses 31 to 37 and think it through for yourself again.

But could the resurrection have been a simple 'mistake?'

There is another theory that the women simply went to the wrong place. They had taken a wrong turning somewhere and, finding an empty grave had missed the real one where the body of Jesus continued to lay.

This idea is based on a careless or deliberate misinterpretation of Luke 24 verse 6. In that passage two angels appeared as 'two men … in shining garments' and said to the women, 'He is not here.' We are asked to believe that this meant, 'You're at the wrong tomb!' Please note that they had spent a lot of time two days before in preparing spices and had observed the tomb where the body lay.[5]

What an insult to women! These poor weak females, over-emotional and suffering from loss of both judgment and memory, went to the wrong tomb because they were clouded by grief! No wonder Jesus was not there. It was simply the case of the mistaken tomb.

This is easily answered

First, they did know where the tomb was. Even in their undoubted and natural grief they had stopped to see where Jesus was lain.

Second, being the tomb of Joseph of Arimathea it was presumably not too hard to find or recognise. It had been intended for Joseph's own burial. He was rich and had obtained permission for it to be used to bury Jesus instead. The tomb would have reflected the affluence of its original owner, with appropriate marks of distinction—including soldiers posted outside! Third, if they were wrong, then the Jewish religious leaders who, knowing the right tomb and being unaffected by grief, would have indicated its whereabouts, produced the dead body, and scotched the Christianity 'myth' once for all!

Fourth, why did over five hundred people claim to meet the risen Christ? Lastly, those who quote 'He is not here' would do well to finish the second half of the verse, so conveniently omitted. It adds the vital explanation why—'He is risen!' Let critics of the resurrection have all the verse or none of it!

Combination theories

Some ideas hostile to the resurrection are variations or combinations of the main four theories. But each is torpedoed by one or more of the following: no remains or body of Jesus were found; for Jesus or the disciples to be willing parties to fraud is inconsistent with the facts; the impossibility of successfully staging the fake resurrection appearances to such a wide and diverse audience; the difficulty of carrying out fraudulent alternatives under such close scrutiny and interest and then to maintain perfect secrecy and silence afterwards; the inexplicable absence of Jesus from the scene unless He rose again and then ascended. Also the twin tests of motive and opportunity applied to the theories, show how fragile they are.

One combination theory that has gained weight with the explosion of Islamic teaching in the West, concerns an imaginative but fanciful suggestion from the 'Gospel of Barnabas,' itself a gospel of straw.[6]

The theory suggests that Judas Iscariot, not Jesus Christ, really died on the cross. God had made him look like Jesus to save a righteous person from undeserved execution. Judas was thus crucified in Christ's place. One can deduce easily, therefore, that it was easy for Christ to appear again because He had never, in fact, been crucified!

It should be said that many Muslim thinkers reject this theory, teaching rather that Jesus swooned on the cross and recovered in the tomb. The Judas theory is, of course, equally wrong as it is based on the concept of fraud. The 'Gospel of Barnabas' is not accepted as authentic by any serious scholar. It only appeared in the fourteenth century and never merited a place in the canon of Scripture, excluding itself because of inconsistencies. Parts of the Koran, which significantly was written later, repeat this view, although other parts of the Koran teach that Jesus died on the cross.

For this view to be true, God the Father and God the Son would have conspired to deceive. Christ's predictions of His death and resurrection would have been false, and His acting as if He had been resurrected afterwards would have been the biggest lie in history. The disciples, who suffered persecution and death for that lie, would also have been either gullible dolts or wicked deceivers. Consider the questions the theory raises. How, where, when and by whom was the substitution made? What is the hard evidence?

We would need to explain why Judas' suicidal death, which took place well before the crucifixion of Jesus, was 'known to all those dwelling in Jerusalem'. The Field of Blood, as it was named, was well known where the hanged body of Judas had fallen and burst open, (probably as a result of having fallen from a branch which broke after having supported the rope which Judas used to hang himself).

All the king's horses and all the king's men
Couldn't put Humpty together again!

No! And neither would they have been able to patch up a dead Judas, and present him to the professional executioners as the healthy Jesus of Nazareth! And then … What happened to the body of Judas afterwards? How was the disposal of his body hushed up? Did it go to the tomb or to Gehenna, outside the city? Why was the tomb empty where Jesus was believed to have lain? Who stole the body? etc. etc. etc.!!!

And again we have to ask how even a non-crucified Jesus could stage his post-resurrection appearances and miracles? He must have had remarkable powers of deception! It makes you wonder why they were not used to escape arrest in the first place, if this so-called Jesus was not determined to go to the cross to die for our sins.

I wonder how the ascension into heaven was staged in front of eye- witnesses. There was not much to hide behind except a cloud as gravity was being defied! But in any case the Bible teaches that the godly do suffer persecution.[7] The supreme example of this is God Himself in the person of the Lord Jesus Christ dying for sinners. The righteous Son of God died for the ungodly. To say that the substitutionary death of Jesus was evaded so that God could save a righteous person from undeserved punishment would be to remove the spinal column of the Bible.

Miracle?

We have looked at four of the usual arguments to explain away the resurrection. Other theories are only mongrel breeds of these four. Do you agree that the theories are weak, inconsistent, illogical, and fanciful? They are as empty as the tomb itself!

There is a fifth alternative! We are not limited to the bankrupt theories of delusion, fraud, swoon or mistake! The process of elimination will cast us on the only theory worth considering: that Jesus rose miraculously from the grave after having paid the price for our sins when He died on the cross. If this is true, we are looking at the most important miracle there has ever been. The whole of Christian belief depends upon it. Without the resurrection, Christianity is not only empty but also deceitful.

Yet we do not need the process of elimination alone to persuade us that His resurrection was a miracle. There are good, solid, examinable reasons for such a conclusion!

To complete this opening chapter, we will look at some evidence to show that it took a miracle. Then each must decide. Was the stone rolled back to let the failed and fraudulent deceiver out? Was it moved so other cheats could make off with a decomposing corpse? Or was the stone removed in order that a world of dying men and women could know that Jesus Christ is alive?

We shall look at the evidence piece by piece. Each is persuasive, but the cumulative effect overpowers all doubt.

The uniqueness of the man who was resurrected

Anti-climax is a terrible thing! It must be difficult for a writer of an action-packed thriller to cap everything else in the story and come up with an even more stimulating, nail-biting and gripping finish! Yet, an exciting story deserves a climactic end! But, you may say, 'that is in the realm of fiction. It would take a miracle to make it happen in fact.'

But, wait a moment. Does not the person and life of Jesus Christ demand a miraculous climax? Do not the well attested facts concerning His birth, life, ministry and death, all of which were prophesied centuries before, lead you to expect a great event to mark the Son of God's prophesied victory over the grave. Could you imagine Him dying of old age, or wasting away under an incurable disease?

The conclusion that Jesus did rise from the dead seems the only logical and fitting climax to His earthly life. Here was no ordinary person! To test that claim, the serious seeker after truth should read, as openly and objectively as possible, the four Gospels which begin the New Testament. They will constantly reveal His dignified demeanour, His warm loving control, His selfless openness, His personal purity which never prevented communication with the worst of sinners, His opposition to religious hypocrisy, as well as His sane and purposeful use of His divine miraculous ability only to glorify His heavenly Father.

There have been more books and songs written about the One who never penned a book or composed a song, than about anyone else. Millions have voluntarily followed Him down the ages, with gratitude and joy. Compulsory and unwilling conscription never enlisted a soldier for His cause! Hundreds of years before the Baby of Bethlehem sanctified the common place where animals fed, details of His birth were foretold and entrusted to writing for all to read. His miraculous conception, normal gestation, and virgin birth declared that here was someone special!

Consider His life. Monastic seclusion was not for Him. Yet He never sinned. He was different. The name of Emmanuel—God with us—could not have been more precise. The prophecy that the son of the virgin would be called Emmanuel in Isaiah chapter 7 verse 14 was fulfilled when Christ was born.[8] His personal and unerring purity, tested in the heated crucible of everyday life and observed by friend and foe alike, convinced cruel Pilate that there was no fault in this Man. His closest followers, who would have seen any inconsistencies in His life, loved and followed Him. They declared Him to be without a trace of blemish. And, as we have already seen, the spy in the camp, Judas, would have revealed any hypocrisy, inconsistency, selfishness, dishonesty or sham. If ever anyone had a vested interest in blowing away the myth it was Judas! What did he do?

He hanged himself in shame because He betrayed the One whom he knew to be good, and whom he knew to be God.

Consider His unsurpassable moral teaching. Where did the carpenter's Son get it from? How did the Boy Jesus confound the wise men at the temple? All the religions in the world are unable to improve upon the Sermon on the Mount. Jesus claimed He came from above. His teaching should therefore exceed all earthly teaching. Did it? Honest doubter, read the Gospels again! Jesus Christ's divinity shines through every page.

His miracles underline His supreme power. God alone could possess that power. See His wisdom in the restrained use of His miraculous power. He was not satisfying idle curiosity, or merely raising a following. Much less to profit personally, as many would have done. Miraculous power was not some toy. The reason? From eternity all power had been His and He was as used to it as a royal prince would be to living in the royal family. See His dignity and grace in acting miraculously and how He constantly seeks to teach God-glorifying truths from it. He never failed, nor expected to! Nature, the storm, animals, inanimate objects, food, the wounded, the sick and crippled, and even the rotting corpse shout to us that Jesus is LORD!

And how about His death? Just on the application of the theory of probability Jesus can be shown to be God. An amazing concentration of prophecies, made when death by crucifixion was not even contemplated, focussed on the dying Saviour at the precise hour of the precise day when God's Passover Lamb was sacrificed for our sins. The tearing of the veil in the temple from the top to the bottom to allow access to the holiest of holies in the temple occurred then. Tombs were split open to mark the miracle of Calvary, and the cross itself was screened with darkness at mid-day. All in Jerusalem were witnesses to the suffering of the Lord Jesus when He was smitten by the holy and wrathful hand of God the Father. He took the punishment of eternity, concentrated into three hours, in His own body on the cross. At that point it was impossible to see the depth of agony that Jesus was undertaking as the forsaken substitute for guilty sinners.

Jesus had foretold His resurrection. He never lied. He was never mistaken. No-one legitimately faulted His morality or the accuracy of His teaching. He fulfilled prophecy to the letter, even on the cross. It would have been incomprehensible and amazing if He had not been raised to live for evermore!

In short, is it not true that only resurrection from the dead fitted the unique conception, virgin birth, perfect life, peerless teaching, fully attested miracles, and miraculously fulfilled prophecies about the death of the Lord Jesus Christ? It was a factual, unique and gloriously consistent climax to a factual, unique and gloriously consistent Person's earthly life!

Confirmed by eye-witnesses

The overwhelming weight of eye-witness evidence confirms that the resurrection was a miracle! But what kind of witnesses were they?

In court, evidence is regarded as strongest when it is presented by a witness who has seen things at first hand, whose testimony is corroborated by one or more fellow witnesses, and who is a person of impeccably good character and reputation. How about the eye-witnesses to the resurrection of Christ? We find hundreds of first hand eye- witnesses. Each one found his evidence confirmed by others. The character of many of these witnesses was such that they turned the world upside-down by their unshakeable faith in their risen Lord. They would die, rather than deny what they had seen and knew to be true. Their moral quality of life was known by all.

But note that these witnesses never set out to prove the resurrection. They had no need to try! It was already common knowledge. None of the disciples were disposed to believe the resurrection and Thomas openly disbelieved it, but these men, who were nearest to the facts, were the very ones who set out to tell us why it happened. They saw no need to say what everyone already knew well enough: that it had really happened.

Remember those changed lives!

At the risk of repetition, we must say again that the change in the disciples after the resurrection demonstrates its reality. Why did they go from fear to faith and from depression to determination?

Their disillusionment, doubt and defeat had melted before the appearance of the risen Christ and the subsequent strength of the indwelling Holy Spirit, like ice cream in a boiler room! How else can one explain Peter's about-turn from three cowardly denials to his bold insistence on the resurrection of Jesus? That same bold confidence in the resurrection of His Lord took him through persecution, to prison and almost certainly to a martyr's grave.

They claimed it was the once crucified and now living Lord Jesus who had changed their lives. They had absolutely nothing to gain from such claims—and a lot to lose. And they were there when it happened!

If we are wrong, explain these facts, please!

Here are a few questions to ask the doubter:

1. Why has the body or skeleton of Christ never been produced?

2. Was everyone wrong who said they had met the risen Christ? As they could not all have been simultaneously deluded, what was their motivation in lying? How did they manage it so consistently and without contradicting each other?

3. What triggered the beginnings of Christianity? No-one disputes the fact that it started immediately after the death of Christ. If it was not the result of ordinary people having met the risen Lord, and joining together to celebrate that fact, what did unify and embolden such a scattered, fearful and diverse collection of people?

4. Why did the early Jewish disciples change the Sabbath day from Saturday to Sunday? They said it was to mark the first day of the week as the day when Christ rose from the grave. Orthodox Jews would resolutely refuse to tamper with the Sabbath. The change of the day testifies to His resurrection.

5. Originally immersion in water (literally baptism) was a pagan rite signifying a change in direction. Why was this rite adopted by the Christian church and given a new significance? Romans 6 verse 4 says 'like as Christ was raised up from the dead by the glory of the Father, even so we also should walk in newness of life.'[9] In short, why did baptism become a Christian ordinance if there had been no resurrection?

6. Why did all the Christians start preaching the Gospel with such earnestness and urgency? If the evidence for the resurrection had been weak, why did they stress it over and over again, especially to those who were closest to that evidence? It was only because of the overwhelming blend of objective evidence and personal experience that they were convinced that Jesus had risen from the dead. That is why they preached and lived with such conviction.

Logic says Yes! To deny the resurrection of Christ is not only to settle on an unbiblical theory of straw, it is also to deny both history and logic as well.

The missing body, overwhelming testimony, change in the disciples, birth and growth of the church, change in the Sabbath, adoption and adaptation of baptism, content and motivation of Gospel preaching: these are weighty arguments. Add the fact that the unique life of Christ demands a resurrection. Remember that no-one argued the case for the resurrection because it was known to have happened, and the inevitable conclusion is that the miracle occurred.

Another miracle!

But there is also an on-going miracle experienced in the life of each individual who turns from the wrong in their life and asks Jesus Christ to forgive, cleanse, and indwell by His resurrection power. Christ can live in your heart by faith. That is a miracle!

I would not write this book myself if Christ had not become my Saviour. Raised in a good loving home, by parents I loved and admired, it was not until the start of my Law studies at University that I turned from my sin and realized that Jesus had been punished in my place on the cross. What a difference it made to yield my life to Him in sorrow and repentance for my rebellion and selfish sinfulness. What a joy to know He lives within my heart today.

The rest of this book could be taken up with personal testimonies of the well-known and the unknown, the rich and the poor, the old and the young. Colour, race and background are no bar to experiencing God's love in Christ. Politicians and sportsmen, blue collar and white collar workers, housewives and widowed, healthy and terminally ill—each one saying, 'He died for me! He rose for me! He lives in me today! He helps me! He blesses me! He guides me! He reproves and corrects me! He forgives and understands me! He answers my prayers! He speaks to me through the Bible! Yes—He rose again and ever lives! And one day I will be with Him in eternity! Won't you trust my living Saviour too?'

The personal miracle begins when you turn from wrong in your life and ask the One who died in your place to take up first place in your heart and life. You take Him with His wonderful forgiveness and eternal life. He takes you with all your sins and weakness!

But the personal miracle continues on day by day as the life-changing truths of the resurrected Christ are applied. Becoming a Christian is like a happy marriage. There has to be the wooing and the wedding! But real love grows as you get to know your Partner well in the days ahead.

As you carefully and personally apply the glorious truth of the risen Saviour to your own life, may you be blessed, changed, and made pleasing to your divine life-Partner. Remember, He loved you enough to die for you!

What next?

The bodily resurrection of the Lord Jesus really happened. What is the purpose of the resurrection and how should it affect my life?

The resurrection:
the credibility of Christ

Did Jesus predict His resurrection? Can we believe what He said?

Who can you trust?

It is hard to believe people you cannot trust! The inner urge to check up on what they say is compulsive. Liars do not make good leaders— especially if you have something to lose.

On the other hand, when you prove by experience that you can trust someone in the most difficult circumstances you will have confidence in that person for the future.

The same is true of a person's actions. Anyone saying one thing and doing something else is dismissed as unstable, dishonest, weak or hypocritical. Consistency in conduct is as important as truthfulness in word.

It is rare to find someone whose deeds and words inspire your full confidence. Consciously or not, we do evaluate those we meet. We decide if we can trust them and follow their guidance or advice. This is as true of buying a second-hand car as it is of saying yes to marriage, choosing a lawyer or selecting a package holiday. It is important that we are not gullible and that we make objective assessments. Sadly too many good-hearted folks have been duped by too many plausible rogues.

There was an interesting test of the authentic prophet in Old Testament times. It was simple! See if what he predicted always came to pass! The response was equally simple—stone him if it did not! That concentrated the thinking of the would-be prophet!

The futures business

Today there are many self-styled prophets, tarot card readers, soothsayers, fortune tellers, Ouija board addicts, spiritist mediums and the like. The futures business is big business the world over. The evil dangers of these harmful practices—roundly condemned in the Bible—are realised too late by some. Lives and homes can be wrecked as Satan uses the old bait of tomorrow's knowledge to hook his catch. Only the risen Christ can liberate us from that hook.

Impeccable track record?

Yet it has to be said that these would-be gazers into the future do not have an impeccable track record. Whilst some alarmingly specific happenings may confirm Satanic intervention, most of the forecasts are so vague and generalized as to be useless. The gullible are taken in. So many do not think clearly or deeply. All are potentially vulnerable who do not trust in the all powerful Saviour and are not firmly anchored in Bible truth. Nevertheless one can dismiss much of this industry as unreliable mumbo jumbo. Think, for example, of the segment of the population whose mothers happened to give birth on the same month that you were born! The horoscopes (better named horror scopes judging by their addictive grip on some who started reading them just for fun) condemn approximately one twelfth of the population to the same kind of future that you will have. What rubbish!

To believe these people and their weird methods you would need to trust their words, actions and character. To have credibility and reliability they must demonstrate a one hundred percent success rate of integrity, honesty and accuracy in fulfilment of what they predicted.

Such people do not exist. 'They never have done,' you may say. But is that correct? Has there ever been someone who was entirely trustworthy, whose words were always true, whose predictions were infallibly realized every time and whose life was consistently and transparently faultless?

Only one person

There is only one contender—the Lord Jesus Christ. Examine in detail His peerless moral teaching, matched only by His life of spotless holiness. Scrutinize the way the long-standing Old Testament prophecies about His birth to a virgin in Bethlehem were fulfilled to the letter. Consider the overwhelming evidence that here was the divine Messiah dying on the cross of Calvary. See the accomplishment to the minutest detail of the specific predictions in Psalm 22 and Isaiah 53. These prophecies were made hundreds of years before death by crucifixion was even known (far less practised). Compare accounts in the New Testament Gospels with these Old Testament prophecies to verify the point!

Some could say that the fulfilment of the prophecies of His birth was pure chance—though the honest mathematician would have to disagree on applying the theory of probability.

Others might argue that His teaching, life and miracles were acted out by Jesus so people would think He was the Son of God. But what a performance! He would have needed to have been divine to have been able to accomplish it so convincingly!

Stage-managed?

Most admit that He could not have arranged His own death to cause these detailed prophecies, (such as Psalm 22), to come to pass. To have stage-managed those details whilst He was dying the criminal's cruel and agonizing death on Calvary would have meant: putting exact words in the mouths of antagonistic scoffers (verse 1); inciting the bestial opposition detailed in verses 13 and 14; enduring dislocation of joints and burning thirst that crucifixion causes (verses 14 and 15); manipulating the piercing of His hands and feet (verse 16); and making the soldiers divide his clothes amongst them whilst influencing them to cast lots for his seamless robe (verse 18). And remember that Psalm 22 is only one of the prophetic sources specifically predicting Jesus' death by crucifixion.

Assume the incredible!

But let us assume the absolutely incredible. Imagine that it was pure coincidence that all this had been done exactly as the Bible had foreseen and declared in the days when execution was by the Jewish method of stoning rather than by the Roman method of crucifixion. Or put it down to some popular (though virtually inexplicable) phrase such as auto-suggestion, (defined as hypnotic or subconscious suggestion proceeding from the subject himself). Although this hypothesis calls for just as much examination and explanation, it does at least sound more intellectually acceptable, even if many who use it do not know what it means or how it works! The more fanciful the theory, the harder it is to have a sensible discussion to test it! Many escape truth through wild assertions thrown out with a mind-flattering title.

Credibility tested by resurrection

Nevertheless, for the sake of argument and purely to assess the credibility of Christ, let us discount the perfect fulfilment of His prophesied birth, life and death. We will judge the credibility of Christ entirely upon His resurrection.

Without doubt, the fulfilled prediction of His own resurrection should settle it forever! If He knowingly foretold His death and resurrection on the third day then His claims stand. Surely no corpse can fix a resurrection! If Jesus rose from the tomb exactly as He had predicted then what He said and what He did could not have been tested more strenuously and we can safely trust Him. Each convinced person would logically and humbly have to ask Him to become 'My Lord and my God' as did the original sceptic, Thomas, centuries ago.

What did Jesus predict?

What, then, is the evidence? Did Jesus predict that He would rise physically again after being crucified? Or was His prophecy for a softer option? Is the now popularised claim correct that the resurrection was spiritual and not physical? If so, the prophecy would have the great advantage that it could be fulfilled without anyone knowing! No-one could prove or disprove it. This form of intellectual escapism might prop up the creaky 'faith' of someone shrinking from being dogmatic and desperately trying to avoid absolute truth, but it could hardly convince a seeking or sceptical world that Jesus in the body was literally raised from the dead. Did Jesus say that He would rise again physically and bodily or not? If He said it, and if He did it, we have no alternative but to take His word as Gospel—literally!

Jesus said 'Destroy this temple and in three days I will raise it up.' He was answering the Jews' request for a sign to establish His authority. Misunderstanding what that meant, they argued that Christ could not destroy the Temple which had taken forty six years to build. But Scripture adds that 'He was speaking of the temple of His body.' It was only after Jesus' resurrection provided the fulfilment of this statement that the disciples remembered what Jesus had said[10] and as a result 'they believed the Scripture and the word which Jesus had said'. Clearly they understood that His prophecy concerned His physical body. The fulfilment of it also led them to believe the Scripture and the word which Jesus had said. A personal faith in the living Lord always leads to vibrant confidence in the Bible—both Old and New Testaments!

The disciples—both ear-witnesses of the promise and eye-witnesses of the resurrection—had no doubt that here was a supernatural accomplishment of a divinely given promise of physical resurrection from the dead.

The sign Jesus chose

Now consider the scribes and the Pharisees. Like many today they were obsessed with the desire to see a sign. They reckoned that this would vindicate His position as the Teacher.

Perhaps many leaders today would have expected a compendium of miraculous signs and wonders to gain the all-powerful Sovereign Lord the popular image He needed to convince a sceptical world! But what was His response?

He referred them to the Old Testament! He pointed them to the historical account of the ups and downs (literally!) of Jonah (thus confirming its historicity). The only sign they would be given was the sign of the prophet Jonah.[11] This shows that Jesus knew He would be raised from the dead physically. After all Jonah was a physical person. The ship, the sailors, and the sea were all physical. A real fish swallowed Jonah. Most importantly, Jonah was delivered from its stomach. After that, he preached God's message in the historical city of Nineveh, whose ruins were positively identified in the nineteenth century. After preaching there with success, Jonah suffered the harmful effects of a burning sun until he sheltered under the physical gourd, that was later destroyed by a physical worm. If Jonah was raised physically then, according to the Lord Jesus Christ, the Son of Man would be raised in the same way.

The verse is simple and clear: 'For as Jonah was three days and three nights in the belly of the great fish, so will the Son of Man be three days and three nights in the heart of the earth.'

Betrayal, death and resurrection

In Matthew 16 verse 21 we are told: 'From that time Jesus began to show to His disciples that He must go to Jerusalem, and suffer many things from the elders and chief priests and scribes, and be killed, and be raised the third day.' This is repeated in Matthew 17 verses 22 and 23: 'Jesus said to them, "The Son of Man is about to be betrayed into the hands of men, and they will kill Him, and the third day He will be raised up".' For the resurrection to be less than physical then everything else in the same context must also be de-physicalised, or spiritualised, including the disciples, Jerusalem, the elders and chief priests and scribes, and His death on the cross. Very significantly, when we take away the physical bodily resurrection of Jesus, we are left with a world of make-believe.[12]

The disciples' reaction to Jesus' prophecy of Calvary and the empty tomb was one of sorrow because of His impending death. Only after that much attested physical resurrection did they remember the glorious prophecy of that more glorious event! How true to human nature.

Overwhelming!

The evidence that Jesus rose again physically, in His resurrection body is overwhelming. It was body enough for Him to eat broiled fish, to be held by the feet, and to invite doubting Thomas to feel His real wounds.

Absolute truth

What can we learn from Christ's personal prophecy of bodily resurrection being accurately and miraculously fulfilled?

Well, is it not obvious? He is trustworthy. If Jesus could get that one 100% 'right,' and never get any other prophecy wrong, and if His life demonstrably manifests integrity and self-consistent honesty blended with unparalleled power, then surely He is THE unique Authority. We can accept His words. Here is absolute truth. The validity, accuracy and reliability of what He says is beyond debate!

I can trust Him

In practical and personal terms I can trust Him as my Saviour, and experience a clean conscience at peace. He who was once wounded on the cross for me, is now risen and living! I must never be ashamed of Him or His words of absolute authority and perfect revelation of the mind of God. I must take His yoke upon me, and learn from Him. I must, by His grace and strength, fearlessly and wisely stand for Him in a hostile world. Ashamed of Jesus? Never! He alone has the words of life! I must follow His command to deny myself, take up my cross, and follow Him. I must heed His last and still binding commandment to go into all the world and preach the Gospel to every creature.

Powerful personal application

But there is an even greater personal application for the Christian. Our risen Lord, the Master-Teacher, has promised to live within each Christian. We have our Teacher always with us, through the Holy Spirit, to interpret His Word, the Bible, to us. He will guide us into all truth through that Word! Followers of great men may claim that their dead heroes live on through their influence and teaching. Some deceived by spiritism or the New Age cult believe the Satanic lie that impersonating demonic beings actually are their dead heroes. But the physical resurrection of the body of the Lord Jesus is our guarantee that He actually lives in our lives by His real, authentic, holy and promised indwelling Presence. My Teacher is with me and within me, speaking to me through His word by the Holy Spirit.

Imagine being in an examination with the expert in the subject legitimately at your side to help! And no cheating!

Yes, Jesus predicted His physical resurrection. His Word is true! Then let us read it daily, trust it daily, and obey it daily as we seek to pass on His truth to others by what we say and how we live!

Practical suggestion

Finally a practical suggestion to help all who have committed their lives to Jesus to live and speak for Him. If you do not already read the Bible systematically and daily, why not start now and ask your risen Teacher to teach you personally His life-changing truth?

Take John's Gospel, the fourth of the New Testament books. Scan it to see where new paragraphs begin. Read one or more paragraphs each day, asking God to teach you and to keep your mind, heart and will open and receptive to what you learn. Ask Him to give you faith in Him and to be obedient to Him.

As you read, note brief answers to the following questions:

What is the main point of this passage?

Can I learn anything about God the Father, God the Son or God the Holy Spirit? What does it teach me about people?

Is there a principle for living as a Christian that I can see here? Do I find, in context, a command to obey or a promise to claim? Is there a good example to follow or a bad one to avoid?

Can I learn how to better follow Christ and be a blessing to others?

Is there anything that God is showing me about myself in this portion?

Finally, what can I turn into prayer as the living Lord speaks to me from His Word?

Prayer

Then turn to prayer—confess your sins, thank God that He pardons them and cleanses you from them in Christ, and ask His help in areas where you need to glorify Him. Pray for your family, friends, and others you meet, that God would bless them and help you to lead them towards Him.

Remember He is the Teacher, you are the disciple, the learner. But He is not a dead teacher. He is trustworthy: His teaching is true. He is the One with absolute authority and power, and has risen from the dead, as He said He would. He is with you to help as you read the Bible and pray. And He will also help you put it all into practice. Trust Him. Commit yourself to His Word and to His care!

The resurrection: was the cross a calamity?

Was Christ's death on the cross a sad tragedy or a saving triumph? What has it to do with the resurrection?

A waste of a good life ?

Why did Jesus Christ die on the cross? Was it: the waste of a good life? Political fickleness? An example of how to suffer wrong bravely? Evil triumphing over good? Do you see a misguided martyr or a starry-eyed idealist's death? Was it a case of this divisive thing called religion? Perhaps it was that Christ's teachings, however nice and loving, just did not work and the Teacher was therefore rejected with them? Was Jesus a failure? Why the cross?

And why do Christians make so much of it? They pen words like 'In the cross of Christ I glory' and 'I'll cherish that old rugged cross.' There must be something positive in it. After all you do not underline your leader's failures when you praise Him!

What the apostle Paul taught

The apostle Paul wrote to the Corinthian church that he did not want to know anything among them except Jesus Christ and Him crucified. Significantly, in that book Paul majored on the resurrection.[13] The apostles were persecuted for insisting on these two things: sinful men were guilty for Christ's death, and, He rose again from the dead.[14]

Paul told these Christians that the double heart-beat of the good news which the Holy Spirit had revealed to him, was the cross and the resurrection.[15] Being steeped in the Old Testament, and especially such passages as Psalm 22 and Isaiah 53, he makes a majestic and simple summary of what he yearns to proclaim: 'For I delivered to you first of all that which I also received: that Christ died for our sins according to the Scriptures, and that He was buried, and that He rose again the third day, according to the Scriptures.'

Thus we can logically deduce that to preach Jesus Christ and Him crucified means that the twin truths of Jesus' work of redemption on the cross and His miraculous resurrection are heralded and explained together.

Back to our first question!

Was it a waste? I heard of a father who threw himself over his young son when he saw that an impact with an oncoming vehicle was unavoidable. Costly, but not wasted. The father died, but the son lived. Paul preached the costly sacrifice of Christ, but the resurrection shows its success.

He knew it would have been a pointless death had it only been to give us an example. In fact our sense of shame and failure would be heightened by the thought that we were so markedly different in our selfishness and cowardice.

If the crucifixion marked evil's triumph over good, then what did the glorious resurrection of Jesus signify?

And how could Jesus' love have failed? It kept Him on the cross. He had power, not only to come down from the cross, but also to erase His oppressors from the face of the earth at a stroke. Yet in humility He hung there, taking their insults and bearing our sins.

Jesus had resolutely and clearly foretold His rejection by men and His death and resurrection. Here was no mere martyr whose ideals proved too big for Him!

And although every Christless man-centred religion does divide and cause friction, Jesus is reconciling men to God and bringing people together at the cross. Even there He is concerned to bring together His mother Mary and John, and to welcome an outcast as guilty as the dying thief into His kingdom.

It is true that the fickle crowd ridiculed the One they had acclaimed such a short while before. But Jesus knew that He would be despised by men and a 'Man of Sorrows and acquainted with grief'. On reflection the crowd may have been surprised at their change of mood, but He was not taken by surprise.

His teaching could only have failed had He not died there. They were right, He saved others but Himself He could not save! He could not save Himself and also be our Saviour. True to His teaching, He had to die if we were to live. That infallible teaching and substitutionary death were gloriously vindicated by the triumphant resurrection.

Some effects of His death

The Bible teaches that there are many effects of Christ's death.

His courageous self-giving in the face of adversity encourages us to seek His strength to continue when we would give up. But example is not the main reason why He died.

His righteousness shines forth against the backcloth of man's meanest and darkest hour of sinful rejection of God. But neither is that the principal purpose of His death.

We did not need the spotless Son of God as a mere martyr because the martyrdom of lesser beings, though sad, is already enough to challenge our commitment. And no martyr, however brave and inspiring, can take away my sin and give me eternal life.

His death showed the fulfilment of Biblical prophecy, both from the Old Testament and from the lips of the incarnate Son of God Himself. It is wonderful to realise its unerring accuracy, but the crucifixion was not necessary to show that! Time and again we see Scripture fulfilled, without calling for the death of the Lord Jesus. So …

Why did He die? What does the Bible say?

I am going to use some theological words. I will explain them simply. They are a bunch of keys to unlock great blessings for you! To understand how a car engine works you need to know a few technical words such as carburettor and alternator. It is just the same if you are to understand God's purpose behind the cross and the resurrection.

Penal substitution

Penal substitution means that a substitute is found to take the punishment I deserve. I have offended God by breaking His laws. I deserve to be punished. That punishment is everlasting, conscious, separation from God. We refer to this as hell—and sometimes we refer to it too lightly. We forget that it is a place of unspeakable torment and irretrievable loss. When Jesus died on the cross, He Who did no wrong took my sins in His own body and was punished by God the Father in my place. He became my substitute to save me from hell. God the Father and God the Son were entirely in agreement that this was the only way that I could escape the eternal judgment I deserved. We see this oneness of purpose in the Godhead when we compare such a verse as: 'God so loved the world that He gave His only begotten Son' with 'the Son of God Who loved me and gave Himself for me'.[16]

Redemption

When a slave was up for sale in the market place, a buyer could come and pay the price. He could do what he wanted with that slave, even give him his freedom. The price he paid was the redemption price. We are slaves to sin. We cannot free ourselves. Jesus paid the price to redeem us when He shed His precious blood on Calvary. When we turn to Him, the risen and powerful Lord, He sets us free as He enters our lives through the Holy Spirit.

A similar illustration applies when someone runs into hard times and takes an article to the pawnbroker who will lend money, against it. To redeem that article its owner has to pay a sum back to the pawnbroker within an agreed time, or it can be sold. Imagine that a generous relative comes on the scene and goes to the pawnbroker to pay back the loan and interest. The article is redeemed and restored to its owner! Jesus paid the price to buy us back to God when we were in the hands of the Evil One. He paid all because we were morally and spiritually bankrupt.

Atonement

I could do nothing good enough to counter-balance the weight of the many sins I had committed. Jesus offered His spotlessly righteous life on the cross in my place. His perfect sacrifice is entirely worthy and so outweighs the combined worthlessness of all my sins. He has atoned for my sins.

Justification

To say God is just means He is righteous. He cannot overlook sin. His holiness demands that it be punished. To take the punishment myself, I should be lost eternally. I have sinned. How can I be declared righteous? Two things must occur. First, my sins must be put on Jesus' account, just as if He had committed them. He must satisfy the righteous (just) anger of God against sin. Secondly, Christ's righteousness (or law keeping) must be put on my account just as if I had been good and holy. When I trust Him, God is then pleased to count me righteous. I am justified as I put my faith in Him, counting only on His death in my place and His righteousness put in my bankrupt account. God the Father demonstrated His satisfaction at this blessed provision for me in Christ by raising His Son from the dead.

Reconciliation

This is an easy concept to understand and occurs in everyday life. When there has been a breakdown of relationships, say between a man and his wife, and a third person brings them together again, there has been a reconciliation. For the sole cause of my sinfulness my relationship was broken with God, Who always loved me notwithstanding my sins. Christ brought me back to the Father when I trusted Him as my Saviour. It has been said that Jesus, being fully God, grasped the Father's loving hand and, being fully man, grasped the sinners guilty hand and brought them together.

If there had been no resurrection ...

Do you ever wonder why Paul, writing in the Corinthian letter under the inspiration of the Holy Spirit, states that our faith is vain (literally: empty) if Christ did not rise from the dead?

Consider some of the results if Christ had stayed dead:

Jesus would have been at best misguided and at worst deceitful—not the infallible and righteous Son of God. His claim to Godhead would be empty.

The Bible would not be the Word of God. It could be put in the fiction section at the library. Christianity would be a mere code of conduct or discipline of legalism—nothing to do with peace, joy and life.

Death would be the endless end. It would have no conqueror. Life beyond the grave would be a groundless dream, and fear of death would reign supreme, for those who dared to think. Remember, no Risen Saviour, does not mean there is no hell, it simply means there is no heaven for sinners. It means God has not provided a Saviour for us.

Those martyred for their faith in Christ would have suffered needlessly, and gained no eternal comfort.

There would be no motivation or incentive to follow Jesus or His teachings—especially in a world hostile to good and to God.

Christ would have accomplished nothing on the cross. No punishment paid, no punishment accepted, only the dread of my punishment still to pay. The redemption price of a failure would have been insufficient and there would have been no power to set me free anyway. Nothing of moral worth could be put into my account, bankrupted by sin, by a failed prophet, mistaken egoist or self-seeking cheat and liar. I could not be counted righteous when the one on whom I relied had failed to fulfil the promise of resurrection. And how could someone not sufficiently in touch with God to get it right reconcile me to God? He could not have been divine.

I could never be right with God. My life would be lived knowing that there is no forgiveness, no cleansing, and no Saviour. This is crucial. If Christ never rose again, I can never be forgiven. If the power of God was inadequate to bring the Son back to life, it is inadequate to create a new and clean life within my heart. If the body of Christ stayed in the grave I must remain forever in the graveyard of sin.

But what a difference the resurrection of Jesus makes!

Just as there is no meaning to the resurrection without the cross, so there would be no meaning to the cross without the resurrection. Calvary would have produced only a remarkable and admirable mixture of brave stoicism, moving martyrdom and super-human courage. The cross of a deceased and conquered Christ could no more give victory over sin than a tomb containing His rotting corpse could conquer death.

But Jesus is risen! He still lives!

By raising His Son from that tomb, God the Father was effectively saying, 'I accept My Son's payment for your sins. I acknowledge that a Divine Sinless Substitute was needed if the effectiveness of that penal substitution on the cross is to last throughout eternity. I know that someone therefore Who was fully man, fully innocent, and fully God had to bear your sins and take the eternity of your punishment on that cross as He became a curse for you during those three darkened hours of judgment. As evidence of My acceptance of His sacrifice on behalf of sinful and guilty people like you, and as My permanent record that My wrath has fallen on Him in the place of those who seek Me in repentance and faith, I have raised my Son bodily from the dead.'

In His own body

Peter tells us that Jesus Himself bore our sins in His own body when He died on Calvary.[17] Yes, in His own body He assumed our wrongdoings, our guilt and shame, and the righteous judgment of God's wrath against them. Literally His body, which had never been a party to sin, was where all the vileness and degradation of our rebellion against God was confronted by God's holy anger. It was punished accordingly—as if Jesus Himself had committed those sins. Therefore it was absolutely essential that in His own body Jesus should be raised from the dead when that penalty had been fully paid. What better way could there be for the Father to demonstrate to the world below and to heaven above that He had accepted the willing sacrifice of His Son's sinless body for sinners than to raise that same body from the grave, and later to heaven itself. That is final evidence in the true sense!

Not only does Christ's resurrection underline His absolutely unique position as perfect man and perfect God, but it demonstrates that He is the perfect Saviour. He will forgive, cleanse, renew, bless, and eternally keep every person who turns to Him.

Here is a brief list, taken from some verses from the Acts of the Apostles, of some of the blessings you may expect even before you get to heaven when you trust the crucified and risen Lord personally:

Acts reference	Blessings for You!
Chapter 2 verse 38	Sins forgiven. You receive the Holy Spirit.
Chapter 3 verse 16	Answered prayer through faith in His name.
Chapter 3 verse 26	He turns you from your sins.
Chapter 4 verse 10	Wholeness spiritually for you as it was physically for the man concerned.
Chapter 5 verse 31	Forgiveness of sins.
Chapter 13 verse 32	Glad tidings from God's promise.
Chapter 13 verse 34	Sure mercies—just as sure as His resurrection was prophesied and accomplished!

What blessings are ours when we commit ourselves to the Saviour Who died for us and rose again!

The resurrection: who is Jesus?

How did the resurrection affect the claims that Christ made?

A crucial question; Who was Jesus?

Who is Jesus? This is of essential and ultimate significance to the Christian message. A clean stream cannot flow from a muddy source. If Jesus is deficient in any way He cannot be regarded as God incarnate. If His teaching, judgment, prophecy, actions or life are suspect then everything He said and did is tainted and open to question. His actions and words will have lost all their validity.

Indeed, if his enemies or critics can cast even reasonable doubt on His credibility, the Christian's faith is seen to be built on the mere sand of optimistic hope.

Once He has been shown to have been deceived, or to have been limited in His knowledge as to the education, culture, or belief patterns of His days on earth, we cannot claim to hear in His words the voice of God speaking through the four gospels in the New Testament. Neither do we see Emmanuel—God with us—but merely some 'carpenter's son' of Galilee.

Mad-man, bad man or God-man?

The position would be even worse than that, if He was deliberately deceptive. If He gained gullible adherents by manipulation or deception, and acquired unmerited credibility and acclaim he would not only have been less than God, He would also have been maliciously sinful.

So was Jesus deceived, deceiving or Divine? There appears to be no other possibility. Either His delusion was so strong that sincere hallucination took Him beyond the fringe of sanity, or His calculated and evil design to mislead others made Him the most despicable fraudster in history, or He was Who He claimed to be. He was either mad, bad, or God.

We will now examine His claim to be God, and see how His resurrection from the dead affects this claim, and the other two alternatives posed.

Before Abraham was I AM

Jesus made no secret of His claim to Deity. He confidently applied to Himself the Old Testament title of Jehovah God when He said 'Before Abraham was I AM'.[18] Those who heard Him knew it could only mean one thing. He was using the name of God as His name. He was telling them He was greater than their patriarch Abraham. Abraham trod this earth before Jesus took on the flesh of the baby at Bethlehem, but Jesus had created the very earth that Abraham had trod!

He claimed that seeing him was seeing God!

When our Saviour said that 'He who has seen Me has seen the Father.' He clearly proclaimed His open secret. 'I and My Father are one'[19] not only referred to their oneness of purpose but also their oneness of being in the Godhead. He acted as the omnipotent, omniscient and omnipresent God.

By definition, God must be all-powerful. If His power could be limited or fettered, except by His own will, He would not be omnipotent. Similarly, the knowledge of God, even concerning apparently hidden things, must be without boundary, unless He chose to limit that knowledge in a specific circumstance. (He is Sovereign and is able to do that!). A partially ignorant being, however powerful, cannot be considered to be omniscient. Did the Man Christ Jesus demonstrate these attributes of Godhood?

His whole demeanour and life-style demonstrated His consciousness of His place in the Godhead. His actions proved His claim, to be omnipotent over disease, demons, men, nature, sin, and over death itself. He demonstrated His omniscience. He knew where Nathaniel was without being told. He knew all about the plot that Judas hatched. The hearts of the inwardly murmuring Pharisees were known to Him. The scribes appeared to be an open book to Him. The detailed background of the immoral Samaritan woman was as obvious to Him as the unspoken problems of His disciples. In His Divine nature He retained all the attributes of God, but as a man He lived and acted as a man. He lived depending and trusting in His Father. This truth is captured in the well-known Christmas carol 'Hark! The Herald Angels Sing' in the lines which explain 'Mild, He lays His glory by. Born that man no more may die.' But although Jesus, the man, was willingly confined to one place at one time as man, yet He was the Son of Man who is in heaven.

He accepted worship

'You shall worship the LORD your God, and Him only shall you serve'.[20] The Lord Jesus Christ knew that to worship anything or anyone other than God Himself was idolatry and would contravene the first commandment 'You shall have no other gods before Me'.[21] In Acts 14, Paul and Barnabas tore their clothes and ran into the crowd crying out their protest that the people of Lystra wanted to deify them after a crippled man had been healed by God through them. They realised fervently that only God must be worshipped. By contrast the Lord Jesus accepted worship unashamedly.

A long string of incidents where worship was given to the Lord Jesus would show that He was always conscious of His Deity because He accepted worship, whether from angels, shepherds, wise men, a leper, a ruler, a Canaanite woman, a mother, a maniac, a blind man, a Roman centurion, a dying thief, doubting Thomas, some Greeks, the apostles, and the whole company of heaven itself!

Did Jesus do what God did?

The theologians say that Christ 'exercised the attributes of Deity.' This simply means that Jesus did what God would do. Of course He did—if He was God! Thus He openly forgave sins—and was accused of blasphemy because, as they show by their question 'Who can forgive sins but God alone?', they knew that His natural exercise of this prerogative marked out His claim to be God.[22]

John's Gospel begins, 'In the beginning was the Word, and the Word was with God, and the Word was God. He was in the beginning with God.' Verse 14 goes on to say 'And the Word became flesh and dwelt among us, and we beheld His glory, the glory as of the only begotten of the Father, full of grace and truth.' John the Baptist, in the next verse, proclaims the eternal pre- existence of the Son in this significant passage, which vies with Hebrews chapter 1 as the clearest statement of the God-nature of Jesus Christ.

In effect, John 1 verse 1 says 'what God was, the Word was.' In other words Jesus is, as Hebrews 1 verse 3 declares, the brightness of God's glory and the express image of His person. We should therefore expect to see Jesus acting in exactly the same way as we see the Father God act in the Bible.

It is worth noting from your reading of the Bible how Jesus clearly showed by His actions and words that He knew He was God: He created, upholds and one day will restore the world; He claimed and demonstrated mastery over creation, including the animal kingdom and the elements; He healed diseases; He conquered evil; He defeated death; He authoritatively presented His teaching as absolute truth from God; He maintained that He fulfilled some prophecy, would fulfil other prophecy and that it spoke of Him; He declared Himself to be the judge of sin; He forgave the penitent; He gave light; He shepherded His people; He ruled history; He lived sinlessly; He would wrap up history when the time came!

How do we know that what He claimed was valid?

So Jesus claimed He was God. He acted and was acknowledged by some to be all-powerful, all-knowing, and all-present when He chose. He accepted worship and was surrounded by it. He purported and was observed to perform the attributes of Deity.

The evidence from all these factors is very strong that Jesus not only claimed to be God but that He was and is God.

Lean over backwards for the sake of argument!

However, just to examine in isolation the influence of the resurrection on His claims, let us lean over backwards and ignore anything else that underlined His deity. Let us accept that any egocentric person can make claims, and that gullible people can be taken in. Let us assume, solely for the sake of argument, that deceived people might have simply demonstrated this gullibility by their worship of Christ, and that by His willing acceptance of it Jesus showed how He selfishly cherished an enormous amount of distorted egoism.

All the evidence of Biblical and extra-Biblical history, and any sane and objective evaluation of the Person, manner, and dignity of Christ, could not so lightly dismiss the overwhelming weight of proof of the character and nature of Jesus Christ. Also, any examination of generally accepted laws of evidence would show just how far backwards we would have leaned to reach such conclusions! But let us ignore that for the sake of argument.

Instead let us ask if there is any one concrete fact that can establish for us that Jesus was not mad, nor bad, but that He was Who and what He claimed to be.

The ultimate test

Surely the ultimate test is the resurrection from the dead. Having clearly and unequivocally foretold His resurrection from the dead, where would Jesus be left if He did not rise again? Either He would be a fallible man, whose prediction had failed miserably[23] or we face a deceitful twister. Anyone who makes fraudulent far-out claims, and attempts to make them appear to be fulfilled deserves rejection not resurrection! Either way He could not be God. Who could confide in an unreliable failure or unprincipled fraudster?

It is true that His moral teaching was of a higher quality and calibre than had ever been produced by anyone else. The Sermon on the Mount showed that. But, unlikely as it is, one might have attributed that to some great fluke or a mischievous gathering together of others' thoughts, dressed up as His own. It seems illogical to most that a larger quantity of lesser thoughts should produce a refined body of greater thoughts, but let us concede this highly improbable point here, just for the sake of the argument.

If His teaching is one sign of His Godhead, His miracles are another. They are even harder to dismiss. But perhaps Jesus' miracles were nothing more than a super-efficiently co-ordinated hoax? (So super-efficient that only God could do it, anyhow!) Or shall we allow, again only for the sake of argument, that the reports were exaggerated (with a remarkably standard degree of exaggeration, it must be conceded!).

Such negative conclusions would certainly go beyond accepted legal guide-lines of what constitutes good acceptable evidence in a court of law, (but we have dealt with that already haven't we?).

So then, just for the sake of argument, we are releasing our hold on the superlative teaching and the widely attested miracles of Christ, just as we have ignored His claims, His acts, His acceptance of worship and His purported exercise of Divine attributes. Now this is a mighty concession to make—even for 'the sake of argument!'

Leaving all that aside, is there any compelling argument why we can accept that Jesus is God, and not mad or bad?

The resurrection suffices!

Yes there is! The resurrection of Jesus from the tomb!

If Jesus Christ really did rise again from the dead then His claim to be God would be fulfilled both in logic and in the power of an endless life. The sealed tomb could not be conquered by a mere prophet, a simple or sincere religious leader, a well meaning martyr, or even a super angel. Only the One Who is both perfect Man and perfect God, as Jesus claimed to be, could rise from the dead in His resurrected body. If it happened then Christ's claim was vindicated. If that, the hardest of the miraculous to achieve, were really a fact, then all doubts must flee.

The biggest and the best-attested miracle on the stage of world events testifies to us the authority, integrity, and power of our risen Lord! We do not need the minor ones, valid as they are! He is risen! He is God! Thomas was right, as his scepticism gave way to reality, 'My Lord and my God!' The resurrection shows He is God, and He can be trusted fully in every way.

'That He might be Lord ...'

The rest of the New Testament emphasises this truth. Romans 1 verses 3 and 4 proclaims 'His Son Jesus Christ our Lord, who was born of the seed of David according to the flesh, and declared to be the Son of God with power, according to the Spirit of holiness, by the resurrection from the dead.' The eternal Son shared the eternal Father's eternal Godhead and nature: the third Person of the Trinity, the Spirit of holiness, witnesses to this by the resurrection. His Deity had been declared before, but the resurrection declares that He is the Son of God with power. Before the resurrection He was in a state of humiliation. After that glorious event are the days of His exaltation. He is not only the Son of God, (which was always true), but with power.[24] Paul again writes: 'to this end Christ died and rose and lived again, that He might be Lord of both the dead and the living!' He 'rose … that He might be Lord!'

As if to emphasise His Lordship, the risen Saviour now accepts worship not only from the now convinced doubting Thomas, but also from the disciples prior to His ascension, and from the angelic host and the occupants of heaven. Truly the once slain and now risen Lamb, the Lord Jesus, is God!

Response

If He then is God, and the resurrection proves it, can we do less than submit to His loving authority in our lives? Can we not trust Him and His mighty power to keep us and bless us as we invite Him to take first place, as we earnestly ask Him to forgive our sins, and as we seek to know and follow Him for the rest of our lives?

'Cleanse me from my sin, Lord.
Put your power within, Lord.
Take me as I am, Lord, and make me all your own.
Keep me day by day, Lord,
Underneath Your sway, Lord.
Make my heart Your palace and your royal throne.'

The resurrection—will there be a day of reckoning?

Is eternal judgment real and, if so, is it avoidable?

Judgment at two places

Punishment for sins can only occur in one of two places. A Christian knows his sins are so offensive to God's holy character that he shamefully admits eternal punishment is justified for those sins. Hell is where the eternal, conscious punishment for those sins is suffered, unless the sinner is saved from it. The only way to avoid this, according to the Christian gospel, is by putting one's faith in Jesus who took the full brunt of divine justice against sin, when He died in the sinner's place on the cross of Calvary.

Sadness and gladness

So the Christian gratefully looks back to the cross of Calvary where Jesus was smitten by God who laid on His Son the iniquity of us all.[25] In sadness and gladness, paradoxically mingled together, the man or woman who has come to trust in the Lord Jesus Christ as the only personal Saviour looks with the apostle Peter to Christ 'who Himself bore our sins in His own body on the tree, that we, having died to sins, might live for righteousness—by whose stripes you were healed'.[26]

The gladiator's triumph cry!

We look at the cross as a place of physical and spiritual darkness, thirst, separation, and rejection.[27] Every person who comes as a guilty sinner to Christ for forgiveness, realises with amazement that Jesus endured all that suffering for him or her individually. He paid the penalty of the punishment for our sins demanded by God's abiding wrath on sin.[28] Like the victorious gladiator who had triumphed in the arena, He cried out emphatically 'It is finished!'[29] Now every repentant sinner trusting in the Lord Jesus Christ and His work on Calvary knows that there is no judgment left against him! Christ has paid it all. I am forgiven and free!

Substitutionary atonement

As God's holy and everlasting wrath on man's rebellion and wickedness, fell on His own beloved Son, nailed as our substitute to that bloodstained cross, we see the Father's amazing love for us. His compassionate love for us is, of course, perfectly matched by the Son's selfless and sacrificing love. Jesus was not an unwilling victim. Two verses, John 3 verse 16 and Galatians 2 verse 20, show us the staggering degree of perfect oneness in the Godhead. The Father's incomprehensible willingness to punish the Son of His love, in my place, mirrors and is mirrored by the Son's determination encapsulated in an old children's hymn which says:

'He knew how sinful we had been.
He knew that God must punish sin.
So out of pity Jesus said
He'd take the punishment instead.'

Have you ever read an account of someone seeking to escape the ravages of a rampant bush or prairie fire? I have heard, more than once, of those who, as the inferno roared onwards, have lit the grass behind them so as to enable the oncoming wind to cause the fire to clear a patch behind them. They then sheltered safely from the approaching flames in that area where the fire had already fallen. Where the fire had struck once, it could not burn again.

In the same way, the only place of safety from the fire of God's righteous judgment against sin is the place where God's punishing fire has already fallen—the cross of Calvary.

The second place of punishment

But there is another place of more hopeless and equally terrible eternal judgment of which the Bible speaks. It is unpopular. Even some claiming to be evangelical have deviated to teachings once claimed by the sects alone, but we have to face the reality of hell. True it defies description. Certainly the picture language of the Bible cannot adequately convey to us the horror of this eternal place where ultimately, consciously, inevitably, finally and in its unspeakable fulness the wrath of God being revealed from heaven against all ungodliness and unrighteousness will be ceaselessly consummated.

Only two choices—wrath or life

Jesus taught that God's wrath abides on him who 'does not believe the Son' and thus that unbeliever shall not see life.[30] A believer in the context of the Bible does not mean one with only mental assent: it refers to one who trusts in, totally commits himself to and wholly relies on Christ. Wrath, for the unbeliever, or life, for the believer, are the only alternatives Christ gives us. There is no half-way house. No second chance. No purgatory. No soul- sleep. No place of diluted reprimand to ease our troubled consciences and calm our fully justified fears. God punishes with abiding wrath unless, repenting, we have put our faith in Jesus and found eternal and spiritual life.

Darkness

Hell is dark. In poetic description, Milton called it 'darkness visible' reflecting a Biblical perspective. It is fearsome, lonely and irreversible—but it is, above all, dark.

If God is light and in heaven itself the Lord Jesus, pictured as the Lamb on the throne, is its light[31] then how dark is that wrathful place of everlasting conscious separation from the eternal Father and His eternal Son!

Darkness in our world often separates, isolates, alienates, and terrifies. Eternal and total darkness separates, isolates, alienates and terrifies eternally and totally. This is not only separation from God and from good, but from anything that would make hell less than hell. The sceptic who jokes that his friends will be there with him stoking up the fires will find it a completely friendless place of abject loneliness. There will be no comfort and sympathy from one's fellow sufferers.

Thirst and separation

And what thirst! In Luke 16 verses 19 to 31, in what could only be a pre-view of hell itself, we see the rich man thirsting insatiably. His raging thirst pictures his hopeless unquenchable desire for forgiveness and deliverance. But it came too late! The 'great gulf fixed' between the eternal destinies of the two sinners—one repentant and other self-righteous—can never be bridged after death. How sad to read that this man and any other, who during their lifetime refused to believe the Bible's truths could not be rescued even by the resurrection of One from the dead! They have never turned from sin and trusted the Saviour. Resurrection proves everything, but imposes nothing on the impenitent, and neither can it relieve eternal, self-pitying remorse.

This separation is massive, penal and final. At the second coming of the Lord Jesus, God's judicial sentence on the unconverted is: 'These shall be punished with everlasting destruction from the presence of the Lord and

from the glory of His power'.[32] And one cannot escape its impact by taking

the false explanation of the (so-called) Jehovah's Witnesses that destruction equals annihilation. When Jesus allowed the woman to anoint Him with precious ointment from her valuable alabaster flask that was first broken, the disciples criticised her and, by implication Jesus.[33] They said 'To what purpose is this waste? For this fragrant oil might have been sold for much and given to the poor.' That word waste is the same root Greek word translated destruction above. The ointment was certainly not annihilated as anyone without a very heavy cold would have been able to tell! The grumbling disciples meant that the precious commodity was irrecoverably lost and forever out of the place they thought it should have been in, the alabaster flask. It was now impossible to collect and restore it to what and where it was before. But whether the word be translated waste or destruction, it significantly and eloquently explains to us what hell is. A place where the soul which has not committed itself into the keeping of the crucified and risen Saviour, by specific and personal repentance and faith in Him, will be finally, irrevocably, and irrecoverably lost. That eternal soul will never be in heaven, because the Only One who could take it there has been rejected.

Jesus as judge

The Bible clearly teaches that Jesus, with His great love to sinners, who would become the repentant sinner's Saviour before death, will nevertheless become the unforgiven sinner's Judge after death.

Jesus wept at the tomb of Lazarus because of the unbelief of those around. He sobbed over Jerusalem because of its unwillingness to repent and seek forgiveness and restoration by coming to Him at His invitation. He had bidden the weeping women lining His redemptive route to Calvary to weep for themselves, and not for Him, such was His compassion for them.

Despite His resolute hatred for sin and inevitable judgment upon it, it seems to me that the Saviour's face will be tear-stained again and His heart be groaning with grief and compassion as He passes final sentence on those who, in a sense, stand self-condemned by sin and hardness of heart. But His holiness and righteousness, which are no less great than His love and compassion, will cause Him to resolutely declare His awesome condemnation of unsaved men and women.

Why will Jesus judge sinners?

There are two reasons why Jesus will judge sinners. First, they have broken God's moral law as summarised in the ten commandments. Hence the indictment that they have practised lawlessness. Secondly, because they did not believe in Him as their Saviour. They could have come to know Him as their Saviour and Lord, but they preferred to control their own lives. That is why the divine Judge's sentencing statement 'depart from Me' is prefixed by the saddest words that can be written across a guilty sinner's life 'I never knew you.'

Religious success and sincerity cannot put off judgment!

How terrible and sad that many to whom these words will be said are 'into religion.' They do things, in the name of Jesus. Some say they perform miracles, do 'wonders', prophecy, or cast out demons. In surprise they will call Him, 'Lord, Lord', as if they knew Him, but they did not know Him, and more importantly He did not know them as His people. Having been rejected as their Saviour, as their Judge He will reject them.

Jesus Will Judge Sinners

And judge He will. Jesus makes that abundantly clear:

> For the Father judges no-one, but has committed all judgment to the Son, that all should honour the Son just as they honour the Father. He who does not honour the Son does not honour the Father who sent Him.
> Most assuredly, I say to you, he who hears My word and believes in Him who sent Me has everlasting life, and shall not come into judgment, but has passed from death into life.

How do the resurrection and judgment inter-relate?

The judgment of the Christian's sins took place at Christ's substitutionary death on the cross. Had Jesus not been raised from the dead we could never have known that God the Father accepted our judgment in Christ. A dead and finished Jesus offers no assurance that the Father regarded the price as paid. A risen Lord is powerful testimony that His sacrifice was more than enough to atone for me.

But is there a connection between the resurrection of the Lord Jesus and the final and eternal judgment of the unsaved?

Yes! First, personal peace comes from knowing that the cup of vengeance filled to the brim with God's undiluted wrath has been drained to the dregs

by Jesus Christ, my substitute, bearing my judgment on the cross.[34]

It is also important that each Christian understands the lost and hopeless state of those outside Christ to galvanise him to work hard in sharing this glorious gospel with those who are unsaved.

However, for some of you who read this, you need to see your peril so that you urgently turn to Jesus.

We can take His word for what we cannot know now!

No-one on earth can testify from personal experience about what constitutes eternal judgment! By definition, it cannot be either eternal or judgment if some human being can say 'I've been through it. I know!' But the One who said He would die and rise again, and did, has earned the right to be completely believed in matters lying outside the realm of our present experience.

The eternity question

Who better to pronounce on eternal judgment than one whose nature is eternal? But if Jesus had stayed in the tomb, or had been dumped like other victims of crucifixion on to Gehenna's burning rubbish heap outside Jerusalem's walls, how could His claim to be the eternal God be justified? The resurrection, proving the God-man's right to exercise the power of an endless life, underlines the fact that the eternal Expert can speak with divine and risen authority on the question of everlasting destruction.

His uniqueness

How many times do you hear, 'Well, no-one came back to tell us!' when discussing heaven and hell? The others have not! Take Mohammed, Buddha, and Confucius and add to them as many popes, rabbis, mullahs, and mediums as you like. None have had a physical bodily resurrection and live never more to die. Include the great politicians, philosophers, writers, teachers and thinkers. Even put in the godly Moses, the Old Testament prophets and heroes, and the miracle-working apostles through whom God revealed His written word. All have gone; except One—His name is Jesus. That is why He has the unique claim to be 'the way, the truth and the life', and why there is 'no other name under heaven given among men by which we must be saved'.[35] He has unique authority, as the only One risen from the dead and ever living, to speak about eternal judgment. Other religious men have their own religious ideas. As the living Lord he speaks the truth.

His righteousness

A good legal system requires the incorruptibility of its judges. Corruptible judges and crooked regimes always coexist. A good judge must be righteous and unbiased. The righteousness of Christ was evident to all through His unrivalled moral and spiritual teachings and His spotless life. He was, indeed, full of grace and truth and universally seen to have been mighty in deed and word before God and all the people.[36] But His resurrection from the dead could not have occurred unless His righteousness was perfect—so perfect that in His risen and ascended resurrection body He would have access to heaven itself without the need of purification.

Such righteousness proclaims that He is the Judge of the earth and shall do right! He is not corrupted by the ravages of time or a sinful nature. He ever lives. He is sinless. Both truths are heralded by His resurrection. This is the whole tenor of the apostolic message in Acts 17 verse 30, that 'God … now commands all men everywhere to repent, because He has appointed a day on which He will judge the world in righteousness by the Man whom He has ordained. He has given assurance of this to all by raising Him from the dead.' All men are sinners and are put on notice that repentance is commanded, otherwise the all-righteous all-knowing risen Judge will find them guilty on judgment day. His righteous standard is assured by the resurrection.

The perfect blend—deity and humanity

The Judge needs to understand God's holiness and man's need. Jesus is fully God and fully Man. His resurrection from the dead means the perfect Man will judge at heaven's bar. He can point to the fact that God's standards are right and that, as Man, He attained them. Had He not risen from the dead He could not be there to vindicate God's righteousness nor to judge man's sinfulness. Because of His obedience in life and death He can unashamedly say, 'My judgment is righteous, because I do not seek My own will but the will of the Father who sent Me.'[37] He never sinned, therefore, He is the only One who can properly be the judge of those who have because God has sent His Son 'in the likeness of sinful flesh, on account of sin: He condemned sin in the flesh'.

A post-resurrection judgment needs a resurrected judge!

Daniel 12 verse 2 declares that all will be resurrected either to everlasting life (by saving faith in Christ) or to shame and everlasting contempt. How can you have such Day of Judgment if the Judge is dead? But Jesus rose again and will judge on that Day. Christians will be judged, for assessing rewards, not punishment.[38] But Revelation 19 and 20 show He will judge the Antichrist, the false prophet, Satan, and sadly and everlastingly all those whose names are not on God's register of having turned to Jesus Christ as Saviour. Is your name in that Book of Life?

Advocate or judge?

Simply stated, we have only two choices.

We should urgently implore Jesus to be our heavenly Advocate now and rejoice humbly in the certainty that we have an Advocate with the Father, Jesus Christ the righteous.[39] With Him representing us, however deep our guilt, we know that His wounds will plead eloquently and effectively for us at the eternal bar.

If however we fail to run to Christ, through neglecting, ignoring, or rejecting Him, we will meet Him as the righteous resurrected Judge who will pronounce the eternal death sentence on us. And we deserve it!

Jesus is not an unwilling Saviour. We need to ask Him now. Condemning Judge, or Saving Advocate? What is He to you now? What will He be then?

The resurrection: bees without stings

Is the Christian justified in facing death with confidence?

The undiscriminating ultimate statistic

The ultimate statistic is this: one in one dies! That takes some contradicting! Death is undiscriminating. Intellect, physical strength, looks, a big bank balance, success, popularity, moral purity, achievement—no combination of these can avoid Death's inevitable knock at the door of life.

Whether Death calls one at a time or claims a crowd in a tragedy, its voice has irresistibly grim authority. It compels towards it those from all backgrounds, colour, creed, and age. Ask any Registrar of Births, Deaths and Marriages! Talk to any undertaker (or 'mortician' as it is termed in the USA—shrouding Death's macabre nature in a cloak of technical manageability). Death is like huge ocean rollers, carrying all before them.

Unpredictably predictable

Death is unpredictably predictable. We know that we will die. We do not know when—three score years and ten is our hope. Yet the summons of Death may be served at any time to any one of us. Every day millions live near the edge without knowing it. A faulty brake lining, an unexpected storm, a terrorist bomb, a fractured gas main, a hidden congenital weakness—any of these may knock at the door of our transiency at their master's bidding.

I well remember one annual company medical. Having been examined myself, I greeted a friend and colleague who was next. I knew him well. I had hired him. He was in vigorous, lively, and fun-loving middle age and about ten years my senior.

We were both later pronounced A1. But he never knew. His results were published the morning of his funeral. Two days after his check-up he started a game of golf he never finished. He died on the fairway.

Fear and bondage

Religious leaders are conquered by death too. Pilgrimages are conducted to some of their tombs. But no-one, apart from the Lord Jesus Christ who rose from the dead, has conquered this last enemy. What a sadly graphic and accurate description of dying humanity is encapsulated in those poignant words of Hebrews 2 verse 15 which describe men and women as being 'through fear of death … all their lifetime subject to bondage.' Only the resurrection of Christ can break that bondage and banish that fear!

Some try to crowd out the reality of that bondage and fear by filling their passing fragile lives with other things. Pastimes, pleasures, plans, ambitions, relaxations! Sometimes legitimate. Sometimes evil. But never able to really liberate! And the uninvited guest nudges with his cold elbow at the most inconvenient and unexpected times and whispers chilling questions to our unprepared soul; 'What is the point of it all? Where are you going? Where will you be in a hundred years time? Are you sure there is no after-life? What happens if there is a God who will judge your sins?'

The sting

Paul, writing by God's Holy Spirit, solemnly declared 'The sting of death is sin, and the strength of sin is the law'.[40] The fear of the unknown can be a terrible tyrant! But, wait a minute! The fear of the known can be far worse! If I am aware that people sometimes get mugged in the city centre at night, I might be apprehensive as I go to buy my burger. But if I enter a dark alley and I recognise a gang of thugs who have been looking for me, that is far more frightening!

And the honest person knows that he is guilty before the God whom he has offended by sin. Shakespeare was right in saying conscience makes cowards of us all! How can someone avoid overwhelming fear when, conscious of flouting God's moral law, he accepts the serious teaching of Jesus that a final day of reckoning must come before a holy and all-knowing Judge? Anyone claiming not to be fearful in that position is a fool, a liar, or both.

The problem solved! Really?

No wonder that the Christian rejoices when he sees that Jesus has beaten death! Since its crushing defeat by the risen Lord of Calvary, death has no answer to the Christian Gospel's rhetorical challenge put poetically and powerfully in the old King James Bible:

O Death, where is thy sting!
O Grave, where is thy victory?

But is death really defeated? Or has its dominion remained unassailable?

Let's be personal. Can I know that if Jesus Christ has become my Saviour I will not go down for the third time in the dark and chilling waters of Death? Have you that absolute assurance, based on solid fact, for yourself?

Why Jesus Christ's resurrection defeats death's dominion

It is only because Jesus died, rose and lived again that He is able to manifest His lordship.[41] That lordship includes mastery over death. Without Christ's having defeated death, the Christian message would be nothing more than a set of morals and ethics set in a background of pious platitudes about God. Like every other religion it would be useless when facing death. But Jesus Christ did rise again from the dead. Because of this there are six main reasons why you and I can personally profit from the blessing of knowing that:

Death no longer has dominion—
Satan's power is broken down!
He has triumphed! Hallelujah!
And He wears the Victor's crown!

1. The sting has been removed

Consider the intense fear of being in a room filled with angry bees. How differently you would feel if you knew, from someone of impeccable trustworthiness and authority, that these bees had no sting. The sting of death is sin: does death still carry that poisonous and painful prospect for the Christian?

By His atoning work on the cross of Calvary, sin (the sting of death) was pulled by our living Saviour. For those who by faith turn from their sin to Him there is no sting of judgment left. God the Father has openly declared this to be the case by raising His once crucified Son! When Jesus left that tomb, death died for those who belong to Him. It became so changed for those who are safely trusting the Lord Jesus that those who die, and go to be with Him, are comfortingly described as having fallen asleep. Contrast this sweet description with that of the unbeliever and their relatives of whom it is tragically said that they have no hope .[42]

2. There is a man in the glory!

Not only has Jesus acted on my behalf on earth in His redemptive and resurrected triumph! He represents me in heaven itself. There is a Man in the Glory pleading for me! Had Jesus stayed dead, this could not have been the case.

But because God has made us accepted in the Beloved,[43] I am as safe in heaven as Jesus is! His everlasting nature, full Godhead, spotless righteousness, atoning blood, and triumphant resurrection mean He is there for certain, for keeps and for me.

Hebrews 7 verses 24 and 25 proclaims that, as the only Priest I need, He continues for ever and that is why 'He is also able to save to the uttermost those who come to God through Him, since He ever lives to make intercession for them'. He could not make that intercession if He did not continue for ever, and He could not continue for ever had He not risen from the dead.

If ever I doubt whether I shall really get through death to be forever with Christ in heaven I need only ask one question: 'Is my Lord Jesus there?' The resurrection and ascension assure me that He is. Thus, sinful and unworthy as I am, I am trusting One who already regards me as justified and even glorified in His sight.[44] In a single transaction my spiritual and moral bankruptcy has been gloriously written off, and I am credited with massive wealth that I never could have earned! A favourite chorus of the soldiers at Sandes Soldiers' Home at Catterick, where I used to love to go to share the gospel, was 'I'm richer than a millionaire just because He cares.' It is true. I am rich because of Him!

3. There is life now in Christ

1 John 5 verses 12 and 13 tell us that he who has the Son has life and that through God's word you may know that you have eternal life. Eternal life is a spiritual life of quality as well as an everlasting life of unlimited quantity. And it is a present possession for the Christian. Although it will last forever, eternal life became mine the very moment that the risen Son became mine.

But how could that be?

First, because eternal life is the resurrection life in Christ which is the birthright of every child of God. Jesus said 'I am the resurrection and the life. He who believes in Me, even though he may die, he shall live'.[45] Secondly, because Jesus is the resurrection and is the life. At the moment I turn to Him I become the instant possessor of the Son and, with Him, eternal life as sure and long lasting as the resurrection of the Lord Jesus!

Not only do I have the resurrected life of the Lord within, but I have the Lord of the resurrected life as well!

4. The resurrection of the body

The Christian's salvation by God's grace will be complete. Not only will we have a saved soul in eternity in heaven instead of the everlasting judgement we deserve, but we will have a resurrection body. When the Christian dies, his soul goes to be with the Lord after his passing through the valley of the shadow of death, however long or short it may be, with the Shepherd (Psalm 23 verse 4). That is why the apostle Paul said he was 'well pleased rather to be absent from the body and to be present with the Lord' (2 Corinthians 5 verse 8) and that he had 'a desire to be with Christ, which is far better' (Philippians 1 verse 23). But God, who prepared an earthly body for His eternal Son to take when He came to earth to redeem us (Hebrews 10 verse 5) will prepare and give us resurrection bodies as well! It will be in these bodies that those alive at the second coming will rise to meet the Lord in the air, when He will be accompanied by those who slept the sleep of death before us and who will be with Him in their resurrection bodies (1 Thessalonians 4 verses 13 to 17). At that time all those Christians who had not gone before to the Lord Jesus, but who are on the earth at His coming, shall 'be changed—in a moment, in the twinkling of an eye, at the last trumpet. For the trumpet will sound, and the dead will be raised incorruptible, and we shall be changed. For this corruptible must put on incorruption, and this mortal must put on immortality.' No wonder Paul writes: 'then shall be brought to pass the saying that is written Death is swallowed up in victory' (1 Corinthians 15 verses 51 to 54).

The argument of 1 Corinthians 15 is that there are different kinds of bodies for differently created creatures. Men, beasts, fish and birds differ.(1 Corinthians 15 verse 39). There are also differences between the celestial and terrestrial bodies, and again between the celestial bodies themselves with the sun, the moon and the stars having their own bodies.(1 Corinthians 15 verses 40 to 42). In the same way God has especially prepared the resurrection bodies we shall have in which we shall know him eternally and enjoy His eternal blessings. Those will be bodies of incorruption, glory, power. They will be spiritual bodies (1 Corinthians 15 verses 42 to 44). We will so much 'bear the image of the heavenly Man' (1 Corinthians 15 verse 49), the Lord Jesus Christ, that the Bible says 'now we are children of God; and it has not yet been revealed what we shall be, but we know that when He is revealed, we shall be like Him, for we shall see Him as He is' (1 John 3 verse 2). What a prospect! What an overwhelming victory over death by the Lord of glory! We do not know exactly what we will be like, but God will give us resurrection bodies so that we can know Him and enjoy Him forever!

5. Heaven promised

Because Jesus rose, you can welcome death as a friend leading you to the deeper and perfect knowledge of the friend who sticks closer than a brother.[46] Like Paul, facing the prospect of death from a prison cell, you can anticipate life ending with gratitude that 'For to me, to live is Christ, and to die is gain.' Unlike some today who teach that our soul sleeps after death, he dogmatically asserted that it was far better to depart and be with Christ. Paul was confident, yes, well pleased rather to be absent from the body and to be present with the Lord.[47]

A confessedly non-Christian ward sister said of a newly converted nineteen year old, with only a few weeks to live, that never before had she seen such a determination to live, but such a readiness to die! That young man had learned the comfort and truth of Jesus' words in Revelation 1 verses 17 and 18: 'Do not be afraid; I am the First and the Last. I am He who lives and was dead, and behold, I am alive for evermore. Amen. And I have the keys of Hades and of Death.'

The resurrection of Christ guarantees heaven for the believer, and the believer for heaven.

6. Satan's grip is broken

We have considered the question of the fear of death and being subject to bondage because of it. The Bible says that the one with the power of death over us is the devil.[48] Christ not only pulled the sting out of death at the Cross, He also won the great battle with that dreadful enemy Satan. Our Saviour died, the Bible states, so that through death He might destroy him who had the power of death, that is, the devil. Had Christ remained a corpse, how Satan would have rejoiced! But in the same way that the resurrection endorsed His victory over sin, it also endorsed His victory over the devil, who previously had the power of death.

In life and in death we can rejoice that:

Jesus is stronger than Satan and sin;
And Satan to Jesus must bow.
Therefore I triumph without and within!
And Jesus saves me now!

He died and rose:

To save us all from Satan's power
When we had gone astray.
Oh, tidings of comfort and joy!

7. We will pass through the valley

Many things on earth will take you into the valley of the shadow of death. But it is only our risen Shepherd who takes us through that dark valley. He alone can do this because He Himself walked that valley and came back as the risen Prince of life. We may share His victory as death approaches.

What a joy to know that I can not only sing 'The Lord is my Shepherd' as a funeral formality but know it as a personal reality, because 'the God of peace … brought up our Lord Jesus from the dead, that great Shepherd of the sheep, through the blood of the everlasting covenant'.[49] Without the Shepherd laying down His life for me and rising again, I would be shepherdless. Like everything else in life, my most precious and prized relationships could only take me to the valley of shadow. But Psalm 23 expresses this strong and quiet confidence in my risen Shepherd:

Yea, though I walk through the valley of the shadow of death,
I will fear no evil;
For You are with me;
Your rod and Your staff, they comfort me.

No mere religious leader can say that to his followers with any credence. The resurrection means we go through death without fear of evil, because the One who conquered the grave is right there with us in the experience of death.

In a three-fold promise in another Shepherd chapter (John 10) Jesus says of His sheep 'I give them eternal life, and they shall never perish; neither shall anyone snatch them out of My hand. My Father, who has given them to Me, is greater than all; and no-one is able to snatch them out of my Father's hand.' See the triple security here: Eternal life ... never perish ... no-one able to snatch out; held by the Shepherd Son; held by the Father! What security for that lost sheep found by the Saviour!

His power was shown in dying for our sins and rising again from the dead. This is the One who had promised: 'I lay down My life that I may take it again. No-one takes it from Me, but I lay it down of Myself. I have power to lay it down, and I have power to take it again.'

This is the power, and this is the Shepherd who will see you through that valley if you trust Him!

The resurrection: is faith a futile fantasy?

Is the Christian in cloud-cuckoo land?

You're fantastic!

❛You look fantastic, Honey!' the young American exclaimed to his beautiful wife. What did he mean? The dictionary is of limited helpfulness! Was she an object of empty fantasy or a non-existent trick of his enthusiastic mind? Or did he mean that, metaphorically only, she was out of this world? For the sake of his marriage I hope he meant the last interpretation of fantastic!

The Christian claims that it is fantastic to know Jesus Christ and His forgiving, life-changing love. He has a living Head who really is larger than life. The sceptic sometimes implies that this is all a question of the Christian's imagination. He contends that it really is a non-existent trick of his enthusiastic mind. Some say that the Christian faith is futile, and therefore fantastic in the uncomplimentary sense because the resurrection of Christ is not factual. Jesus did not rise again from the grave. The Christian is therefore in cloud-cuckoo land!

The Bible says the sceptic is right!
The Bible agrees with the impeccable logic of those who, based on the premise that Jesus stayed dead, disputes Christianity's claim to be absolute truth. Cloud-cuckoo land should indeed be stamped in big letters on the believer's spiritual passport if Christ did not rise!

Advice to atheists, agnostics, and antagonists!
If you want to flatten Christianity, start at the resurrection. Some have already tried! Some from other religions with no risen Lord draw their battle lines here. The New Age tries to philosophise it away. If you can destroy that great root of unique Christian teaching, the tree of faith cannot stand.

Pussy cat or tiger?
But be careful! You are not crushing a kitten! You are tangling with a tiger! It will get you in the end if you persist with open combat. One highly intelligent lawyer set out to write a book disproving the resurrection and concluded by writing *Who Moved The Stone?* The first chapter was entitled 'The book that refused to

be written!' Frank Morison had been convinced against his inclinations by the sheer weight of evidence as he logically set about disproving the resurrection.

Why does faith minus resurrection equal fantasy?

Why would faith be fantasy if Christ had stayed in that borrowed tomb? Look at logic to answer this question. It involves, amongst other things, the god who got it wrong, the pointlessness of the cross, Christian experience being merely psychological, death being alive and well, unity in the graveyard, and no heaven!

The god who got it wrong

Do I believe that Jesus Christ is God (with a capital G)? Certainly! Well, if He did not rise from the dead He was a god (with a small g) who got it very wrong! He had prophesied His own resurrection. If He failed to rise that was a Gaff with a capital G!!

The pointless cross

Is it my belief that Jesus died for my sins on the cross and paid the price of my rebellion when He took my eternal judgment in three hours? Emphatically, and gratefully, yes! Fair enough, you might say 'but if His claim to be the risen Lord was flawed, how can you be sure that He was correct in describing Himself as "the Son of Man who came to give His life a ransom for many"? Perhaps He got that wrong too—and no-one has paid sin's penalty in your place.' There is no evidence of the Father's satisfaction with the Son's sacrifice if He did not raise Jesus from the dead in powerful recognition and acceptance of it. In fact, the death of the Son of God on Calvary's cross would have been pointless.

My experience only psychological?

How about the psychological possibility if I do not possess a risen Saviour living within me? This experience, without a factually raised and living Lord, is nothing more or less than psychological. It would be of equal interest, but of no greater validity, than any other experience produced by drugs, drink, hypnotism, hysteria, ESP, or transcendental meditation. The follower of the New Age would have every right to put his heightened self- consciousness the same as my conversion—neither experience would have any basis in fact! If Jesus Christ really died and rose again I can count on His risen and powerful indwelling as I turn from sin and ask Him to be resident and President in my life! But if it is found to be a hoax—or even just a hiccup—then I am in a crowd of millions who down the ages deceived themselves into thinking they each become a new creation in Christ.[50]

Death is alive and well!

Do I rejoice in the defeat of arch-enemy death by the Victor from the sealed tomb? Christians would reply in the words of the Easter hymn:

Death could not hold its prey!
Jesus my Saviour!
He tore the bars away!
Jesus my Lord!
Up from the grave He arose
With a mighty triumph o'er His foes.
He arose the Victor from the dark domain
And He lives forever with His saints to reign!
He arose! He arose!
Hallelujah! Christ arose!

What a let-down if death defeated Jesus and lurks to torture every doomed follower of their failed Master! I had better start worrying about the pointlessness and shortness of life again.

Unity in the graveyard

Do I regard Christianity as unique among religions because Jesus is unique, especially in His resurrection? But if Christ is not risen, Christianity becomes merely another try your best religion, with no hope offered to the dejected failure, no comfort to the dying, and no certainty to the unsure. Without a resurrected Lord, Christianity is merely competing with other man-made systems of religious observance or philosophical invention to pull at its own boot strings to vainly try to lift its followers to God. This would have the unifying effect among world religions that some seek, but the greatest unity is in the graveyard. All are dead there!

No hell? ... no heaven?

Some who want to dismiss the possibility of final judgment will, no doubt, endeavour to take comfort on the basis that they have decided that the resurrection never happened. They would argue that if Jesus is not the risen Judge sitting in the Court of Eternity, then we can escape from our guilty blame without punishment. Perhaps that is the ultimate reason why so many rationalise their prejudices and conveniently decide that there was no resurrection? 'After death the judgment'?[51] Many long that they could live and die, and go to nothing. They reason: 'No resurrection of Jesus—means there is no Christianity—means there is no judgment.' But what a false comfort. No Saviour does not altar the fact of sin, it simply means the certainty of hell, the absolute assurance of no heaven. If Christ is not risen, He certainly cannot welcome us into a heaven He Himself could not reach!

In 1 Corinthians 15, perishing, not annihilation, is the only alternative to resurrection. Paul argues that without the resurrection, they would still be in their sins. Therefore the terrors of hell would await them. This would mean, he says, no Saviour, no sins forgiven and no alternative to a lost eternity. He does not support the erroneous view that when you're dead, you're done for.

Eliminating the resurrection is therefore not a clever intellectual way of rescuing the perishing. It effectively sinks the lifeboat.

Bullets for the enemy?

One further evidence for the resurrection needs to be made here. Paul, with all New Testament writers, writes assuming the resurrection. Did Paul give bullets to the enemy, or shoot himself in the foot by resting the whole case for Christianity on the factual bodily resurrection?

Please read 1 Corinthians 15 and ask:

Would Paul ruin Christianity? Paul makes statements that would ruin Christianity if Christ were not alive. Why, if the evidence to support his argument for the resurrection were not overwhelmingly strong? It would be making ammunition for the enemy!

You may have heard of the modernist preacher's note to himself in the margin of his sermon notes—Weak point so shout loud! But Paul does not shout loud. He carefully and deliberately asks the very question he would fear if Christ were not alive. Truth will never melt under the searchlight of honest investigation, like chocolates in the clammy hand of an excited child. The Gospel has nothing to fear, and everything to gain, from being questioned by sceptics or sincere seekers. Jesus said 'Seek and you shall find'.[52]

Final futility of faith—if no resurrection

Paul announced to the world at large that Christianity was futile if Jesus Christ did not rise bodily from the tomb. He exposed what some must regard as the soft under-belly when he stated:

If there is no resurrection of the dead, then Christ is not risen;

If Christ is not risen, then our preaching is vain, and your faith is also vain; Yes, and we are found false witnesses of God;

Your faith is futile; you are still in your sins;

Those who have fallen asleep in Christ have perished; We are of all men most pitiable .[53]

At least no-one could accuse Paul of being blinkered! He certainly looked at things from the other fellow's point of view, yet remained convinced of the truth of his message.

The nature of the Christian gospel

The quotations cited immediately above do, in fact, show the true nature of the Christian message of forgiveness, the new birth and eternal life. This discounts forever cardboard Christianity with no resurrection, no miracles, no supernatural intervention in the affairs of man, and no directly inspired and infallible revelation through the Bible. The great apostle is emphatic that there is no authentic Christianity without the intervention of God through the glorious resurrection. Without it, all is lost. How some Ministers and Bishops who promise to defend the faith dare try to demolish these and other doctrines we cannot imagine. They suggest either this is a merely symbolic teaching and that Jesus stayed dead or, it just does not matter what happened. How can they claim to be Christians, however sincere some of them undoubtedly are? With the New Testament's insistence that the cross and the resurrection are the essential foundation of Christianity's unique message of redeeming and saving love, how dare others purport to give hope beyond the grave through their rituals, through man's own efforts in good works, or by simply being religious?

Abundantly plain

From the few verses quoted from 1 Corinthians 15 the Bible makes it abundantly plain that without a personal faith in the risen Lord Jesus Christ:

We remember a dead failure, not a risen Lord (verse 13);
Those who preach are empty and have nothing worth saying—hot air about heaven, you might say! (verse 14);
All Christians are liars (verse 15);
With our futile faith we cannot escape sin's power or penalty (verse 17);
After death there is no hope and there is no comfort to give anyone facing death (verse 18);
There is no-one anywhere in the world to be pitied more than a Christian! (verse 19) He is not only helpless and hopeless, he has fooled himself! His living Hope and his eternal Help is a decomposed body!

Faith would be a futile fantasy if death had conquered Christ. None of the precious benefits of His resurrection would be real. Christians for 2000 years would have to admit to being deceived and having deceived. Worse still, the impostor whom they mistakenly followed would have been doubly indictable on the same charges!

Reverse the doom and gloom!

But Jesus Christ is alive! He did rise from the dead! There can be no honest doubt remaining for anyone who openly considers the evidence.

How wonderful that, in verses 20 and 21, Paul follows the section we have looked at by the glorious and manifestly obvious truth:

But now Christ is risen from the dead, and has become the firstfruits of those who have fallen asleep. For since by man came death, by Man also came the resurrection of the dead.

This means that, like a pilot tug guiding the liner into port, He has gone before and guarantees a future resurrection for all those linked to Him by faith.

Now turn on its head the depressing list of 'doom and gloom' compiled on the purely hypothetical basis that the historical and factual resurrection had not happened. See how mightily effective is the resurrection of the Lord Jesus in validating and making productive the simple personal faith I put in the Son of God who loved me and gave Himself for me:[54]

Not only has Christ risen but the Lord of glory has become my personal Saviour and Friend! (verse 13);

The Christian alone has an absolutely meaningful and wonderful message which has first transformed his own life! Listen to any party political broadcast and ask, 'Will this message have value to me in one hundred years time?' and 'Has the message changed the politician inside?' (verse 14);

He who declared Himself to be the way, the truth, and the life[55] has shown us the truth about Himself, which is glorious, and the truth about ourselves, which is humbling. Putting those truths together, as led by the Spirit of truth in accordance with His revealed truth in the Bible, we have turned from our falsehood to Him. He has truly become our Saviour. We discover within a desire to turn away from lies, dishonesty, and deceit. We know both the truth about God and the God who is Truth. This knowledge has liberated us and we become concerned to share it with others who need Him. (verse 15);

Life would really be futile without faith in the only One who can make it meaningful now and eternally. Having died for our sins and having been raised from the dead, He has saved us from sin's punishment in hell, He does save us from sin's power on a daily basis, and He has promised to save us from sin's presence in heaven. (verse 17);

Death has ceased to be the enemy to end all that is good. Instead I can welcome it as a friend who will usher me into the eternal presence of my living Lord! (verse 18);

There is no reason to pity the Christian. The poorest is richer than a millionaire! The weakest is stronger than the world's strongest man! The least known is the King's Son! The least intelligent knows the most important things! The most sickly is in bountifully good health! These are not in the physical realm, of course, but are what every Christian possesses spiritually, and therefore eternally, in Christ who conquered death! (verse 19).

How about your faith?

All this leads to a personal and vital question. Is my faith a futile fantasy or has it been put in Him who died for me and rose again? Am I looking unto Jesus the Author and Finisher of our faith?

It does not matter how big or small, or how strong or weak your faith is. Don't compare it with your neighbour or minister. What really matters is where you put it! Naturally it needs to be nurtured day by day. It will grow stronger as it is nurtured in your daily walk with Christ. Important to this growth in spiritual health and strength are: a careful daily reading of your Bible and praying over what you read; spending Sunday, the Lord's Day, profitably including going to hear the word of God clearly taught in a fellowship of Bible-believing Christians; and getting involved in serving Christ especially telling others about your Saviour.

But let us get the horse before the cart! Your faith in God becomes valid only at the point where you confess your sin to Him and turn from it to Jesus who died in your place, asking Him to enter your life as your living Saviour and Lord. At that moment, however falteringly, you have put your faith where it counts—in Him! The only important question to ask yourself is 'Is all my trust for my forgiveness only in this crucified, resurrected and ascended Lord Jesus Christ?' Trust Him now if you have not already come to know Him!

A prayer

Yes, do it now! You can use the timeless truths of a wonderful old hymn, quoted, which focuses on Jesus as the Lamb of God who takes away the sins of the world :56

My faith looks up to Thee,
Thou Lamb of Calvary,
Saviour Divine.
Now hear me while I pray;
Take all my guilt away;
Oh let me from this day
Be wholly Thine.

Saving faith

If this is your heartfelt prayer you will know God's grace and forgiveness in your life. Reality will replace futile fantasy. Your faith cannot save you in a vacuum but you will find that it is the channel of forgiveness for you as you place it in Jesus Christ. This is what we call saving faith, and is portrayed throughout the Bible. Here are some passages dealing with it:

By grace you have been saved through faith;[57]

Believe on the Lord Jesus Christ, and you shall be saved;[58] Whoever calls on the name of the Lord shall be saved;[59]

As many as received Him, to them He gave the right to become children of God, to those who believe in His name,[60]

If you confess with your mouth the Lord Jesus and believe in your heart that God has raised Him from the dead, you will be saved. For with the heart one believes to righteousness and with the mouth confession is made to salvation.[61]

Christians are not presumptuous when they speak of being sure they are forgiven and are going to heaven. Faith is not a futile fantasy. Assurance is one of those wonderful comforts for the believer on his way ever nearer to heaven. It can be yours as you trust in this living Saviour.

The resurrection: the indwelling Trinity

Can I know the Trinity is true? Or are the 'Jehovah's Witnesses', Mormons and New Agers right?

A crutch?

Have you ever heard that, religion is a crutch for the weak? Lenin called it the opium of the masses. This suggests that a weak-willed, or otherwise inadequate individual discovers within himself a religious- shaped vacuum. He invents or adopts a religious solution to fill it. To change the metaphor, He leans on the infamous religious crutch to prop him up. The truth of the religious solution is utterly irrelevant. What matters is that his inadequacy has been met.

Magnanimity and absolute truth

With apparent magnanimity and understanding, those who hold this view allow the Christian his belief in a Triune God and a risen Saviour, as long as it meets his perceived need. By the same token, they would object to the evangelical insistence that the Bible is the only infallible, inerrant and complete revelation of God and that the Lord Jesus Christ is the absolute truth. The apostolic message 'Nor is there salvation in any other'[62] is anathema to them. One objector said to me 'There is no such thing as absolute truth!' He was, of course, demonstrating the obvious confusion and implied contradiction of his position. One cannot deny the concept of absolute truth without using the very same concept!

Objective reality?

What does the resurrection teach us about the objective reality of being indwelt by the Lord Jesus Christ, and therefore by each of the three Persons of the Trinity—the Father, the Son, and the Holy Spirit? Is this really taught in the Bible? Is it real in Christian experience today? How is it affected by the resurrection of the Lord Jesus Christ?

Trinity under attack

The doctrine of the Trinity has always been under attack from cults and modernistic teaching which dilutes or denies the supernatural elements of the

Gospel. It still is. God's truth will never be popular in a hostile world. What, briefly, is the Trinity?

There is only one God. The Bible teaches that God the Father is God; the Lord Jesus Christ is God; the Holy Spirit is God, and, like the Father and the Son, He also is a Person, not just an influence or power. These truths are found in Scripture like sugar in tea. They permeate the whole and give it that sweet flavour of divine truth. Occasionally we find a passage which may be likened to the bottom of a cup where there is undissolved sugar. Here the teaching is particularly concentrated and easy to taste. God the Father, God the Son, and God the Holy Spirit: One in Three and Three in One. That is the clear Biblical teaching on the Trinity. The fact that such a truth transcends the capability of man's feeble mind to understand it does not mean that the same feeble mind should not accept it. On the contrary, we should willingly bow to the divine Mind expressed in Scripture. The Trinity is not the only thing beyond our comprehension that we accept as a fact!

The resurrection and indwelling

Never do you see the truth of the Trinity more clearly in life and in action than when you consider the indwelling of the believer by the God who has saved him. And the resurrection of Jesus is fundamental to this consideration. Without the risen Lord there could be no indwelling Saviour. God's guarantee of meeting our needs is underlined by what the Father, Son and Holy Spirit do for me and in me when I turn to the risen Lord. Without the resurrection of Christ the whole doctrine of the Trinity, and the assurance that every child of God becomes a human temple where God lives, would be merely another mystical or esoteric theory.

What makes someone a Christian?

What is a Christian? What makes him distinctive? How does he differ from sincere adherents to other religions?

Is it that he does good things? Clearly this cannot be the case, since some non-Christians live exemplary lives and help others. Is it that he has been through certain ceremonies, like baptism? But others have their ceremonies that touch the outward man without changing him from within. Both prisons and parsonages have incumbents who have undergone such ceremonial initiations yet whose lives deny any claim to be following Christ. Do we need religious observances, like regular churchgoing or repeating certain prayers? Again, the world is not far wrong when it says that some churches are full of hypocrites.

An example from the Bible to help our thinking concerns the thieves who died on the crosses next to Jesus. Both were criminals, they reviled Jesus, and were morally and spiritually bankrupt. Neither could go through a ceremony or perform good works. Neither could do anything to get right with God. They were hopeless—until one turned to Jesus, recognising he had sinned and failed. That alone was why Jesus told him that he would be with Him in paradise that very day. He still had done nothing better than the other unrepentant thief. It was Jesus who saved him, not anything he had done or undergone.

But perhaps it is a philosophical perspective that makes me a Christian? But the world does not lack philosophers, and the Bible does not teach that Christ came to make us philosophise. In fact the apostle Paul deliberately rejected the world's philosophies as a means of salvation so that he could concentrate on preaching the message of the cross.

Three descriptions of an authentic Christian

It needs to be said that a committed Christian will do good things, that Christian baptism will be important to him, and that he will observe certain godly habits to help him in his Christian walk, such as attending a Bible-believing church, reading God's word daily, and regular and personal prayer. He has a philosophy of life, but this will be drawn from the well of God's inspired truth, the Bible. But these things are the result of his having become a Christian, and not the route whereby he became a Christian.

There are three descriptions of what it means essentially to be a Christian which concern my relationship with each Person of the Trinity.

Temple of God

In 2 Corinthians 6 verse 16 the believer is described as the temple of God. The context is verse 18 where the LORD Almighty says: 'I will be a Father to you, and you shall be my sons and daughters.' In this quotation God, whose temple the believer has become at conversion, must be the Father. Thus when I believe in Christ as my risen Saviour, God the Father, the LORD Almighty actually takes up residence in me so that my body becomes His temple! The thought is simple though staggering in its consequences.

Temple of the Holy Spirit who is in you

In 1 Corinthians 6 verse 19 the challenging question is posed: 'do you not know that your body is the temple of the Holy Spirit who is in you, whom you have from God, and you are not your own?' So the Holy Spirit Himself dwells within you. Interestingly, verse 20 goes on to say: 'For you were bought at a price; therefore glorify God in your body and in your spirit, which are God's.' After repentance from sin and turning to the risen Jesus who bought you at a price, you are now described both as one whose body and spirit are God's and also as possessed by the Holy Spirit. So if my body is the temple of the Holy Spirit and if at the same time it belongs to God, then who can the Holy Spirit be except God? Through conversion to my living Lord Jesus, the third Person of the Trinity, God the Holy Spirit, has moved in and He owns me!

Christ in you, the hope of glory

I have already shown the overwhelming evidence for the deity of the second Person of the Trinity, the Lord Jesus Christ. God's gracious indwelling of the believer in Christ both underlines that key truth and demonstrates the reality of the Trinity. In Colossians 2 verse 6 the Christians at Colosse were said to have received Christ Jesus the Lord. The same believers had earlier been taught that the riches of the glory of this mystery among the Gentiles was summarised in the phrase 'Christ in you, the hope of glory.'[63] As the late Professor Verna Wright, the eminent rheumatologist and founder of United Beach Missions, once said: 'What is a Christian? Strike out the letter "a" and you have it! CHRIST IN! A person who can truthfully say that I have "Christ in" my life is a Christian!' Turn again to John 1 verse 12, to see the truth endorsed: 'as many as received Him to them He gave the right to become children of God, even to those who believe in His name.' To 'believe in His name' means to trust Him for Who He really is, the Saviour God who became man for us. As we trust Him, we realise that 'Christ in you the hope of glory' becomes a reality.[64] Who but a Saviour who had conquered death could come to live in my life? But it is God in His fulness who enters when Jesus becomes mine.[65] The Father takes up residence; the Spirit lives within; Christ moves into my life—when I turn to the living Saviour!

Two or three witnesses

The Bible exhorts us to get two or three witnesses to confirm a testimony under investigation. This principle has passed into our legal system. We will accordingly examine passages from Romans, from Ephesians and from John's Gospel.

First witness: Romans 8 verses 9 to 17

In this passage we have various statements of the indwelling Father, Spirit and Son. All are used interchangeably and in the same context. Compare the phrases below and ask yourself 'Who dwells in the Christian?'

the Spirit of God dwells in you;

if anyone does not have the Spirit of Christ, he is not His; Christ is in you;

the Spirit of Him who raised Jesus from the dead dwells in you; His Spirit dwells in you;

you received the Spirit of adoption whereby we cry out 'Abba, Father';

The Spirit Himself bears witness with our spirit that we are children of God.

Father, Son and Holy Spirit all claim the title deeds to our lives, without dispute among them, and have already moved in as the sovereign Triune Lord!

Second witness: Ephesians 3 verses 14 to 21

Again simply consider two phrases below from the verses mentioned above:

'be strengthened with might through His Spirit in the inner man, that Christ may dwell in your hearts through faith'

'that you may be filled with all the fulness of God.' Question One: Who is in the inner man? Answer: His Spirit.

Question Two: Who dwells in our hearts? Answer: Christ. Question Three: Whose fulness may fill me? Answer: God.

There is only one God, but the Spirit, the Son and the Father are inseparably One in Person and purpose to bless those who have yielded to the Lord of the empty tomb!

Third witness: John 14 verses 16, 17, and 23

In the above references compare these words of Jesus:

I will pray the Father, and He will give you another Helper, that He may abide with you for ever, even the Spirit of truth ... He dwells with you and will be in you;

If anyone loves Me, he will keep My word; and My Father will love him, and we will come to him and make our home with him.

The Spirit, the Father and the risen Son—each One individually and together agreeing to inhabit the Christian! But there is only One God!

Were you converted three times?

Before examining what devastating effect the failure of Jesus to rise from the dead would have had on the Trinity, there is a stupid question to pose! The answer sheds a light on the Trinity as it relates to my conversion.

The question is 'Were you converted three times?' Silly as it seems, this question has to be answered by those who seek to deny the Biblical teaching about the Trinity. If I do not believe that God the Father, God the Son, and God the Holy Spirit are One, then I have to explain how am I indwelt by each of them! The born-again Christian believes that at the moment he turns from sin, realises that Jesus has paid sin's penalty for him on the cross, and hands his life over to his risen Master, he was immediately indwelt by God who is One in Three, and Three in One.

But those who deny this truth are confused on this point! If there is no entity in the Godhead and yet I find the Father, the Son and the Holy Spirit each living within me, presumably each must have had His separate and individual entry. Put another way—I would have needed three conversion experiences! Did I trust Christ on Sunday, with a 33.3% indwelling? Then on Monday achieved two thirds of maximum as the Father came in. If so, presumably on Tuesday the Holy Spirit finished the job off and the God-head had moved in completely— the instalment plan of salvation! The principle is that if there is no Trinity, and I am now indwelt by three distinct Persons, then I must have been converted three times! How ridiculous and how un-Biblical. As soon as I exercised saving faith in the substitutionary death and triumphant resurrection of Jesus, I became the dwelling place, as described above from the Bible, of God the Father, God the Son and God the Holy Spirit. The risen Saviour is God my Saviour and Emmanuel, God with us, who has promised never to leave or forsake His own. His name JESUS, which means Jehovah is Saviour, was rightly given to Him because He was the One to save His people from their sins.[66] This He did through His redemptive death and His miraculous victory over the empty tomb!

Where would the Trinity be if no Resurrection?
It is not at all surprising that those who deny the Trinity also deny the bodily resurrection of Jesus. Be they followers of the cults such as Jehovah's Witnesses, Christadelphians, New Agers, an imaginative renegade Anglican bishop, or a sincere but misguided follower of Islam, (who at least is consistent!) To admit the resurrection they must accept the Trinity! If they accept the Trinity they cannot deny the resurrection. No surprise that they decide to reject both!

No title deeds and insufficient consideration
With no resurrected Christ, God the Father would never have a just and legitimate right to take possession of the house of my life. He would have no title deeds. He could not have regarded the price paid on Calvary by His Son as sufficient consideration, and so did not raise Him from the dead.

When He enters the life of the repentant and believing sinner it is to stay, satisfied that the price for full vacant possession has been paid. His Son's blood ensures He is no unauthorised squatter.

The coming Helper
At one point our Saviour said: 'I tell you the truth. It is to your advantage that I go away; for if I do not go away the Helper will not come to you; but if I depart,

I will send Him to you.'[67] Jesus said this before His prayer at Gethsemane, before His ordeal at Calvary, before His glorious resurrection, and before His ascension to His Father. Clearly the Helper, the Holy Spirit, would not come into the believer's life without the ascension, and the ascension required the resurrection. Once risen from the grave and ascended to His Father, Jesus was then ready to be represented by the third Person of the Trinity. Every person who now prays for forgiveness and exercises faith towards the Lord Jesus is immediately filled with the Holy Spirit. Christ enters by the Holy Spirit at that very moment. That is why God tells us 'if anyone does not have the Spirit of Christ, he is not His.' So the resurrection of Christ permitted His ascension, which led to the Spirit's ministry of entering the lives of every blood-bought sinner exercising faith in God's mercy and grace through the death of His Son.

Indwelling by life, not just by teaching

God the Son rose again from the dead! Thus He can now take up residence through the Spirit in the hearts of believers. A dead Saviour has nothing to offer.

Some may argue that a master-teacher, great leader, or popular celebrity may live on after his death by his teachings—or his recordings—in his most dedicated and devoted disciples. If they mean it in a literal sense they are either on the verge of insanity, or living in an unreal world, or are dangerously influenced by the evil of spiritism, or a combination of all three.

This claim that the hero lives on is a pale, limited, lifeless, and powerless thing compared to the indwelling of the ever living Lord Jesus Christ, whose resurrection is as much a historical fact as His birth, life and death. People say that Hitler lives on. They mean his teachings influence people. The matchless teachings of Jesus do influence even those who do not know Him as their Lord, but we are not looking at influence but indwelling.

Far above the wonderful influence of His words, as the Spirit of God still uses them today to convict, convert, comfort and challenge men and women, is the miracle of His actual indwelling presence in the life of anyone who turns to Him. Jesus can so enter and transform a life that, with the apostle Paul, one can experience and proclaim, 'I can do all things through Christ who strengthens me'![68] The rotting corpse of a failed teacher could never do that! In words from the same letter, we can experience the peace of God, guarding our hearts and minds through Christ Jesus. No wonder Paul rejoices that 'For me to live is Christ, and to die is gain' nor that, having come to know the risen Christ, his aim is now to better know Him and the power of His resurrection.[69] He cannot spend enough time with the living 'lover of his soul!'

Thank God for the resurrection!

Purchased by the indwelling Father! Possessed by the indwelling Spirit! Empowered by the indwelling Son! Title deeds with vacant possession for the Trinity! All this is mine because Jesus died in my place and rose again. I can know the eternal Godhead living in my life now, and be sure that one day I shall share eternity with the great God who loves me so. Thank God for the resurrection!

Back to those crutches

So my Christian experience is not merely my choice from one of several lightweight alternative crutches to help me limp along, rather a personal and dynamic experience of the Lord of glory in my life. This is no psychological make-believe that happens to fit the shape of my perceived need. It is an all-embracing new life centred around my risen Saviour and controlled by His love and power. It is founded on the historicity of His birth, life, death, resurrection, ascension, and Godhead.

Paul put it this way: 'I have been crucified with Christ; it is no longer I who live, but Christ lives in me; and the life which I now live in the flesh I live by the faith of the Son of God, who loved me and gave Himself for me'.[70] Christ had conquered the apostle's life just as surely as He had conquered the tomb! Resurrection life had transformed both!

Examine yourselves

The Gospel does not ask anyone to become a little more religious. It insists that you turn your back on your sins and the right to live your life your way. You vacate the inner throne, and humbly welcome the living Prince of Life to rule with His peace, pardon, power, presence, purpose, and principles. And then one day, maybe soon, He promises that you will meet around His throne in heaven!

Can you wonder why God is concerned to say to us 'Examine yourselves as to whether you are in the faith.'[71] he asks each one of us to be very sure that Jesus Christ is in us.

The resurrection: Will Christianity crumble or will Christ come again?

How does the resurrection relate to the second coming of the Lord Jesus Christ?

Joy

❮ And the disciples were filled with joy and with the Holy Spirit'[72] is an amazing commentary! Their joy existed, despite being persecuted by the Jews and put out of Antioch by the chief men and devout and prominent women.

This had been preceded by the rippling effect of the spread of the Gospel throughout all the region. We know from the rest of Acts 13 (especially verses 28 to 41) that the message they had proclaimed concerned four interconnected subjects: the Lord Jesus Christ, His death, His resurrection and 'through this Man …' the forgiveness of sins. The disciples' evangelistic endeavours and daily lives so centred on the risen Lord of Calvary that they were filled with joy and with the Holy Spirit. No wind of adversity could shake that God-centred joy! What a change from the previously dejected bunch of beaten and leaderless individuals.

Four priorities of the early church

Earlier, as recorded in Acts 2 verses 30 to 36, it had been business as usual for them. They had been declaring the message of hope and forgiveness that the publicly recognised and well-attested resurrection of Christ was bringing to each person who turned to Him. We read in verses 40 to 47 what happened to those who became Christians. Four specific priorities are listed among their continuing and steadfast activities. They emphasised the apostles' doctrine (God's word), fellowship (sharing of themselves in a disciplined but new-found openness), prayers (they now found it natural to meet together and pray out loud naturally). Before commenting on the last important constituent of their spiritual life and growth, we should note that whenever Jesus Christ has first place it will be marked by specific spiritual desires and actions. These will always be headed by personal and group Bible study, genuine and spontaneous fellowship with each other, and a personal life of prayer that leads to a natural expression of it in the group context. The early church was characterised by its outgoing witness to seek the lost. How did they do it? Because, first and foremost, they concentrated on a right relationship with their risen Lord and with each other. The basis for evangelism was real, spiritual and active.

Breaking of bread

The other activity, third in the list of four, was the breaking of bread. This was done from house to house each day. (They enjoyed their daily fellowship together. Each day they were also with one accord in the temple.) An insight into their joyful fellowship and infectious faith is given also in verse 46 which tells us that they ate their food with gladness and simplicity of heart. Gladness! Again we see the hallmark of joy, even as they met together to break bread. That their meetings included more than just having food is equally obvious. 'Breaking of bread' is one of four spiritual activities.

So what does breaking of bread entail? 1 Corinthians 11 verses 23 to 26 give a clear and simple explanation. By eating the broken bread we remember the One who said 'Take, eat; this is My body which is broken for you; do this in remembrance of Me.' By taking the accompanying cup we recall His words 'This cup is the new covenant in My blood. This do, as often as you drink it, in remembrance of Me.' The Christian remembers that at Calvary the enormity and vileness of his sin caused the spotless Lamb of God to be separated from God the Father and to bear the punishment of the judgment of his sins. He recalls with feeling and gratitude that the blood of Jesus freely flowed to cleanse his sins.

Looking backwards. Looking forwards

The breaking of bread commemoration was therefore a remembrance that Christ had died for their sins. They looked backwards to the wonderful work of redemption on Calvary's cross. But it was much more than that! It was an emphatic and prophetic proclamation that Christ would come again—a spiritual telescope looking forward to His glorious second coming. Verse 26 explains 'For as often as you eat this bread and drink this cup, you proclaim the Lord's death till He comes.' As they broke bread, recalling that the body of the Lord Jesus was broken on the cross for their sins, they were also assuring each other and declaring to all that 'Christ will come again!'

Gladness out of sadness

The remembrance of the death of a loved one would normally be marked by overriding sadness. Yet Jesus Christ's death was remembered with gladness.

Why? For the same reason that they spread the Gospel and lived their lives with joy. Christ had risen! Jesus was alive! The living Lord of glory had promised He would return! They knew that 'at the name of Jesus every knee should bow, of those in heaven, and of those on earth, and of those under the earth, and that every tongue should confess that Jesus Christ is Lord, to the glory of God the Father.'

Resurrection and ascension

But Paul preceded his inspired and inspiring statement of confidence in Christ's second coming by reference to His death and resurrection. He explained that Jesus became obedient to the point of death, even the death of the cross and then heralded triumphantly 'Therefore God also has highly exalted Him and given Him a name which is above every name.' Scriptural truth, irresistible logic, and resurrection triumph are interwoven in this unique message of Christianity! When you ask Paul why he was so sure that Christ would come again in universal triumph and to universal acclaim, he teaches us that it is because God has honoured His death on the cross by raising Him from the dead and granting Him a place at His right hand on high.

No resurrection means no ascension means no second coming; no sensitive mixture of grief and gladness in celebrating His death; no awe that the altogether lovely one has been punished for our sins. But the Father has highly exalted Him, and His glorious return is as sure as His resurrected life in His people now. So gladness and joy prevails.

Miraculous resurrection—magnificent return

Little wonder that, writing to the Thessalonian Christians Paul reminds them how they 'turned to God from idols to serve the living and true God, and to wait for His Son from heaven, whom He raised from the dead, even Jesus who delivers us from the wrath to come'.[73] The historic fact that Jesus was raised from the dead is underlined immediately after the reminder that they wait for His Son from heaven. It seems as if Paul is effectively saying 'Your future confidence in His coming to earth again is built on the rock- solid assurance and the certainty that Jesus rose again.' His miraculous resurrection ensures His magnificent return!

The dead rise and the living are caught up!

Perhaps the most joyful anticipation of the Lord's second coming is in 1 Thessalonians 4 verses 14 to 18. Consider some words from that passage; 'God will bring with (Jesus) those who sleep in Jesus … we who are alive and remain until the coming of the Lord will by no means precede those who are asleep. For the Lord Himself will descend from heaven with a shout, with the voice of an archangel, and with the trumpet of God. And the dead in Christ will rise first. Then we who are alive and remain shall be caught up together with them in the clouds to meet the Lord in the air. And thus we shall always be with the Lord.'

Resurrection bodies for all believers!

What a prospect! What promises! Christ will come again with the souls of those who have trusted Him and fallen asleep in death. At His shout they will be reclothed with resurrection bodies which will rise to be with Him in the air! Then Christians who have not died will be changed into their new resurrection bodies in the twinkling of an eye and be re-united in the clouds, not only with those whose bodies were lately sleeping the sleep of death, but much more importantly, with the coming King! We will be with Him in this joyous, pure, loving, powerful relationship forever! Well may we exclaim 'Praise the Lord!' Had He not conquered death there could have been neither resurrection nor resurrection bodies in which those who are saved will enjoy eternity.

Bed-rock of certainty

In our anticipation of ecstasy let us not forget the bed-rock of certainty guaranteeing this coming miracle of future history. Verse 14 says 'if we believe that Jesus died and rose again, even so God will bring with Him those who sleep in Jesus.' Did you note the words 'if we believe that Jesus died and rose again?' What is the guarantee? Simply this—'Jesus died and rose again.'

It is foolish to speculate on future details. But we can have full confidence in one who conquered sin, defeated death, and rose triumphantly to ascend majestically to heaven, from where He will return in sheer glory and splendour.

Is Christianity crumbling?

Is the Church still persecuted? Do Christians fail? Are there sad and hypocritical inconsistencies in the churches? Are followers of Christ sometimes taken up with the wrong or unhelpful things of this world? Do I ever despair of my own coldness and selfishness? The answer to these questions is, sadly, yes. But does all this mean that Christianity will crumble? No, Jesus is the Lord of history. He is saving men and women, boys and girls. He is moving the great nations of the world around to suit His purposes. The events of history are simply the scaffolding around the great work that the Lord Jesus is doing in the world. He is building His church. Nothing in earth or hell can stop Him. When He has finished all He intends to do, He will wrap up the heavens like a cloak, and come in power and glory as the Judge of all mankind.

Ashamed

Shamefaced, we Christians have to blush and whisper that we are a miserable bunch of failures in many ways. Someone has called the church a sinners' club. It certainly is! But the Sinners' Friend has called us into it. We do wander far from Him at times. We often do not do what we ought to, and just as often do what we ought not to do. We do not resemble our selfless Saviour in the least. We are ashamed. If the future of Christianity depended upon us, it would crumble, as we ourselves have so often done.

He is in control!

But Christianity is Christ! Happily for sinful mankind the future of the Gospel of God is with its Maker. Jesus will return, as King of kings and Lord of lords, and in power and great glory! His resurrection from the dead declares it. Just as sure as He is alive, He will come again! He will have the last word in history. He is in charge. He is never taken by surprise. He will come in perfect harmony with the infallible Divine timetable. He will come to bless eternally. He will come to punish everlastingly. What about you? Are you ready for His coming? Are you living for Him until He comes, or calls you?

'Beloved, now we are children of God; and it has not yet been revealed what we shall be, but we know that when He is revealed, we shall be like Him, for we shall see Him as He is. And everyone who has this hope in Him purifies himself, just as He is pure.'

The resurrection: is it pie in the sky when you die?

How about heaven?

Healthy, wealthy and successful?

There is an undue and over-dramatic emphasis on being healthy, wealthy, and successful amongst Christians today. Success and power are higher up the agenda than service and holiness.

Rejoice in what He has done

Over-exaggerated accounts of miraculous exploits side-track keen but immature Christians and cause rightful reticence in discerning non- Christian thinkers. This emphasis has led some to think that our rejoicing should be on the basis of what God enables us to do rather than what one day He will cause us to be in Christ. We rejoice not in what we fancy we have done for Him, but in what we know He has done for us in His substitutionary death for our sins and the sharing of His glorious resurrection in our lives.

Ultimate privilege and crowning glory

Today's success, however spiritual, may fade away into tomorrow's failure, but can the gilt-edged security of the risen Christ's blood-bought promise of eternal life ever be devalued? Certainly not! The euphoric seventy who 'returned with joy, saying, "Lord, even the demons are subject to us in your name"' had their priority refocused when Jesus said 'do not rejoice in this …, but rather rejoice because your names are written in heaven.'[74] The ground of rejoicing is not in gifts or successes but in the certainty of a relationship with Jesus.

For Christians, heaven is the crowning privilege and certainty. All else that I have, am or do is relatively insignificant, however important from my earth-bound perspective.

Can I be sure of heaven?

But is it just pie in the sky when you die? Someone has wryly, (even cornily!), remarked that pie in the sky when you die may be acceptable to a hungry pilot whose plane and parachute have both failed, but it is not much good to someone facing the real issues of life and death! It is vital to know if heaven can be a certainty for me.

Exclamation mark!

And it is at this point that the resurrection of the Lord Jesus Christ becomes so significant. It stands between earth and heaven like a glorious golden exclamation mark lightening the dark and lowering skies of doom and doubt, and pointing dying men and women to the living Hope.

What I know about mountain climbing could be written on the side of a postage stamp, rather than on the back! But I have observed that the first one to the top helps the others up. Jesus is the first one to the top! He is not only willing but also able and in position to get us there too! Our risen Saviour is already in heaven as our representative, friend and sympathetic high priest. He is at work for us.

Nutritious Roman sandwich!

Romans 8 verses 34 and 35 is like a crusty sandwich of two questions with a meaty and nutritious answer between; 'Who is he who condemns? It is Christ who died, and furthermore is also risen, who is even at the right hand of God, who also makes intercession for us. Who shall separate us from the love of Christ?'

Feelings of guiltiness continue, because I still sin against the Lord Jesus. See there how the condemning accusation thrown against my fragile feelings of assurance, is answered by my confidence in a crucified, risen and ascended Saviour. Note also how any suspicion of doubt that, after all, I may end up separated from God is answered by those same assuring facts: Jesus Christ died for my sins; He rose bodily from the grave; He now lives at the right hand of the Father on high; He pleads there for me. Christ who died, and furthermore is also risen is my answer! My risen Saviour also makes intercession on my behalf. Even as I live below, shamefully at times in selfishness and sin, He ever lives to make intercession for me![75] Because He conquered death He presents in heaven the invincible argument for my forgiveness—Himself! He is there in His once crucified but now glorified resurrection body, wounded for my sins and raised for my justification.

Yes, the resurrection guarantees my place in heaven because He is already there!

What is heaven?

But, what is heaven? It is where the forgiven sinner can gaze upon his loving

Saviour in the perfect bliss of glory! It is very hard for us to appreciate because the concept of eternity and the comprehension of perfection are light years beyond our experience. But it is real, and could never be better. Paradoxically every second of eternity will seem even more glorious than the one before, even though the second before was unbeatable! Every thought of self and sin will be overwhelmed in the worship of the One who fills eternity with His glory. That worship will be a perfect and ordered blend of emotion and logic, ecstasy and reason, personal meaning and objective truth. It will centre on the only Person who can ever say 'Do not be afraid; I am the First and the Last. I am He who lives, and was dead, and behold I am alive for evermore. Amen. And I have the keys of Hades and of Death.'

Prepared place—home and worship

Prior to His death, resurrection and ascension Jesus said, 'In my Father's house are many mansions; if it were not so, I would have told you. I go to prepare a place for you. And if I go and prepare a place for you, I will come again and receive you to Myself; that where I am, there you may be also.'[76] In Revelation 21 verse 23 He is described as the Lamb, the very light of heaven. He died as the sacrificial Lamb of God. He rose as the living Lord of glory. In heaven His death and resurrection are evident as we are told that there 'stood a Lamb as though it had been slain' who is worshipped by heaven's redeemed and angelic throng as they say with a loud voice:

Worthy is the Lamb who was slain
To receive power and riches and wisdom,
And strength and honour and glory and blessing![77]

Without that resurrection there could have been no return, no mansions, no worship, no redeemed, and no heaven for them. But there was a return, there are mansions, there is worship, and the redeemed share heaven with the angels that did not sin. The redeemed have an ingredient of gratitude in their singing to the Lamb, that those angels have never experienced!

No wonder that the 'First and the Last, who was dead, and came to life'[78] who is rightfully and gloriously centre-stage, invokes the response from the twenty four elders in heaven, that they fell down and worshipped Him who lives forever and ever.

Resurrection body

We saw earlier that at the moment of death the Christian's soul immediately goes to be with Christ. We also touched on the fact that our bodies will be raised.

Jesus' resurrection body was body enough to eat fish, manifest real wounds, and to offer Thomas the opportunity to touch it. In Glory itself, Christ's presence is central through His resurrection body.

Logically, the only way that I can see Him and enjoy His presence forever in heaven is to be on His wavelength—that is, to have a resurrection body too. As one would expect, Scripture meets and supercedes this piece of impeccable logic.

The Inheritance kept for me!

We have seen that 'when He is revealed, we shall be like Him, for we shall see Him as He is.'[79] Whether your own path to heaven will be by being changed in the twinkling of an eye at His second coming as your earthly life is instantly translated into a heavenly one, or by being changed as one of the dead ... raised incorruptible,[80] the Lord will give you an entirely new resurrection body. Some have described it as a spiritual body. Peter tells us that not only is there 'an inheritance incorruptible and undefiled and that does not fade away, reserved in heaven for you' if you are a Christian, but you will be one of those who are kept by the power of God through faith for salvation ready to be revealed in the last time! The God who will have kept your inheritance for you, also will have kept you for your inheritance! How will He keep you? Now—by the power of the risen Lord in your life! Finally—by giving you a resurrection body in which you will enjoy eternity!

It is not surprising, therefore, that Peter also exclaims and explains 'Blessed be the God and Father of our Lord Jesus Christ, who according to His abundant mercy has begotten us again to a living hope through the resurrection of Jesus Christ from the dead!' His resurrection is the key to our confidence.

The heavenly Man

Paul argues in 1 Corinthians 15 that we shall rise because He rose. In verses 47 to 49, we see that, just as we share Adam's flesh of humanity, we shall share the same type of resurrection body as the Lord Jesus: 'The first man was of the earth, made of dust; the second Man is the Lord from heaven. As was the man of dust, so also are those who are made of the dust; and as is the heavenly Man, so also are those who are heavenly. And as we have borne the image of the man of dust, we shall also bear the image of the heavenly Man.'

Hallelujah!

My risen Friend and Priest pleads in heaven for me now. One day He will welcome me there as I worship Him who died and lives for evermore. His atoning death, vindicated by His risen life, has saved my ever-living soul. One day He, who is the Resurrection and the Life will give me a resurrection body like His, the heavenly Man.

Because He rose bodily from the grave, I will rise in a new body to be with Him in heaven! Well may we sing:

Up from the grave He arose
With a mighty triumph o'er His foes.
He arose the Victor from the dark domain
And He lives forever with His saints to reign.
He arose! He arose!
Hallelujah! Christ arose!

The resurrection: which religion is real?

Only two religions in the world? Questions, Questions!

Which religion is true?

'How can I tell which religion to follow when there are so many in the world?'
'Time is too short to try them all out and find out if there is one that is right.'
'Surely all religions lead to God. As long as you're sincere, you're O.K.'

You will have either heard such questions and comments, or even made them! The man in the street is bewildered by the choice, and being ignorant of the contents of each of the many religions, gives it up as a bad job.

He hears sincere adherents extolling the virtues of their own brand. Or they are so vague that he is at a loss to find out what they believe. Others confuse him saying that they are all really the same, despite some basic teachings that clearly contradict each other. Too many, too bigoted, too vague or too confusing—these are the problems that face even a sincere seeker after truth. They certainly provide a convenient shield for those who are looking for an excuse for not seriously considering what happens after death.

Is there a single right religion? How do I know when I have found it?

Confusion and unity

As already indicated, this confusion is not limited to those without a settled conviction. Some try to bring together all the world religions, and a myriad of individually concocted ones also, into an all-embracing set of beliefs, in the hope that unity will demonstrate truth. This could include something as widely accepted as the ecumenical movement, as potentially sinister as the New Age movement, or as genuinely confused as an honest Joe who does not like to see division and conflict. The discerning person realises that you cannot have truth or unity where the parties concerned sincerely and firmly hold teachings which exclude beliefs held by others in the so-called unity.

For example, Muslims will accept neither the Trinity, nor the Deity of Christ, nor His substitutionary death on the cross for sinners. To them the resurrection of Jesus is a myth. Clearly there can never be religious unity between Islam and Biblical Christianity whilst they hold these views, though one would hope and strive for personal harmony and mutual respect.

Similarly no grounds for unity exist between someone who believes that Christ is sacrificed at each Mass and the person who accepts that Jesus on the cross paid the first, last and only sacrifice for sins. Other fundamental differences between Roman Catholicism and Biblical Christianity which will always prevent a true spiritual unity include the worship of Mary, prayers to the saints, purgatory, the priesthood, confession, and the authority of the Pope.

A person may even say he is a protestant, but deny the authority of the Bible as God's word. He cannot have a true unity with someone who takes the Bible as the only and complete source and final authority.

So unity is not a matter of having a single letterhead! Who, then, has the truth? Muslims, Hindus, Buddhists, Confucionists, followers of Baha'i World Faith, Mormons, 'Jehovah's Witnesses', Christadelphians, New Agers, some other sect, or Christians? And if you select Christianity, is it to be Anglican, Methodist, Baptist, Brethren, Congregationalist, Pentecostal, Presbyterian, Nazarene, Free Evangelical, or what? With such variety how can an honest seeker ever find out if God has revealed any definitive truth?

The existence of God

Leaving aside philosophies that basically focus on the inner self most would agree that the common factor in all religions is the existence of God. Any religion that does not hold that God exists is, by definition, atheist. We will not find God in its philosophies, however complicated, or in its heightened awareness of self, however flattering that may be to a lost and guilty humanity. So we will assume that we are looking for the God who is.

How would God let us know?

Let us assume that God exists, cares for His creation and wants us to know about Himself. We will also take as read that He desires that we should worship and walk with Him, and is concerned that we learn how we can come to know Him. Assuming this, it is logical to conclude:

1. He will not confuse us with contradictory teachings about Himself, and how we can know Him. Any element of confusion cannot come from Him;

2. He will reveal Himself clearly, permanently, unchangeably and with authority;

3. His revelation will differ fundamentally from any attempts of man to explain by their religions what God is like, and how we can know Him;

4. He will be right, because He will deal in absolute truth. They will be at best only partly right, because their knowledge is limited;

5. If He is holy and loving, and man is in rebellion against Him we would expect that truth to be about a remedy and that man will be largely antagonistic to it.

We might also add that each man-made religion is likely to have some points in common and some points at variance with each other. They may share some points with God's revealed will, but will certainly differ on the most fundamental points.

Is there a 'diamond' on the pebble beach?

We are spoilt for choice and do not have the time to go through every religion, systematically examining each one in detail. Life would be too short. Rather we should ask if there is one contender which is distinctively different from all the others. If we find such a candidate we should examine that one. We need look no further if that one is the truth, since all contradictory beliefs are false. As we rightly expect God to reveal Himself clearly and distinctively, this method of approach would appear to be logical, honest, and economic in time. If you find the ideal wife you do not register at a lonely hearts club! If you find a missing diamond on a pebble beach, you do not examine the remaining pebbles!

Man-made religion says I can contribute

All religions encourage us to believe that we can do something to get to know God. Perhaps by something we do, or by something done to us, a ceremony. For some, finding God is finding self. Some follow philosophies which have just enough of the supernatural about them to scrape in under the title religion. Others persevere under great suffering, or work hard to improve, hoping for a better life in the future—either the next time round, or in the after-life. The choice is large. There are almost as many variants of religions as people. The central principle for all religions is that I can 'Do it my way,' I can at least contribute something. One would expect the true religion, if it exists, to be distinctively different.

Religions spread uncertainty

Another common factor amongst religions is that very few claim a fixed assurance of unshakeable acceptance by God. Acceptance, access, or knowledge of God is rarely, if ever, known, and if reached, is very difficult to maintain. Being sure is hard work, staying sure is even harder. Uncertainty is a hallmark of man-made religion. Uncertainty of full forgiveness, of full acceptance, of heaven. Like Scrooge looking at his gravestone we ask, 'Must this be?' Hopefully, the diamond among the pebbles on the beach would offer certainty.

Religions are powerless

We do not need creeds and codes, but cleansing and changed lives. There are plenty of philosophies and props, but where is the purity and power? Religions are all alike. Surely we would discover distinctive realities in that different religion not available amongst the others on offer.

Religious leaders are themselves passing failures

Most important of all, we see that the leaders of all the worlds' religions were men of clay. The best were failures—some even admitted it. Not only have they failed through personal sin, but they have all fallen to the last and worst enemy of lost mankind, Death. Tombs of great religious leaders attract interest and pilgrimages. Death has defeated them. Few claimed, and none demonstrated, bodily resurrection. None claimed substitutionary death for failed men and women, in which God's punishment against sin was borne vicariously for others. None claimed and demonstrated, by a spotlessly sinless life and a glorious resurrection from the dead, to be the God of eternity coming through a virgin birth to take on Himself the flesh of humanity. None will extend their influence in eternity. Those who still live will die soon. In one hundred years, where will they be? Where the others are! If there is a truly God-given religion, its leader will excel over the heads of other religions in his nature, character, power, holiness, love, achievement, and durability.

Look at the diamond!

But does the unique diamond of God's true revelation exist among the religious pebbles on the world's beach? Biblical Christianity has distinctive claims. Its followers claim there are only two religions in the world. One is man-made, humanity's self-help solution, appearing under many distinctive names. The other has been revealed by God through the written word of God, the Bible, and the living Word of God, the Lord Jesus Christ. This diamond glitters from its many facets to reflect authoritative and infallible inspiration from God. It is not just another pebble on the beach of world religion. It is God-made, God-revealed, God-executed, God-given, and God-guaranteed. How different! The historic and wonderfully unique resurrection of the Lord of glory underlines its fundamental difference from the mere ideas of men.

Compare biblical Christianity with other religions. We have seen above the factors common to man-made religion:

You must do something, but you cannot be sure whether you have done enough;
Codes of religious conduct or philosophy cannot give power and motivation and produce joy and peace in keeping it;
The leaders are temporary sinful human beings.

Remember those five marks of God-given rather than man made religion?

They were: non-contradictory teaching; clarity of authoritative revelation permanently and unchangeably recorded; fundamental difference in teaching from other religions; certainty of absolute truth; likelihood of being opposed by sinful men.

How does biblical Christianity compare?

The Bible's unique consistency and authority

From internal and external evidence, archeological discovery, fulfilled prophecy, and its power to change individuals and nations the Bible substantiates its claim to be the word of God. It is inspired, infallible, and complete. It is examinable in thousands of languages. God has made sure it is the best seller. It was not written by one person. It has no man-made mist of mystique conveniently produced to prevent objective examination. It reflects the writings of over forty authors, varied in cultural position and educational background, in several original languages written over approximately a two thousand year period, at numerous geographical points. The scope for thousands of contradictions is enormous. Yet there has never been one proven fact to contradict the Bible, neither can an in- context supposed contradiction be upheld. The Bible is more than a book— it is a court room where all the sixty six books, like witnesses, lay themselves open to the cross-questioning of sceptics and seekers. Here is no one-sided view of one man or small group, but objective testimony that any court of Law would accept. Here is God the Holy Spirit speaking through His fallible servants to produce an infallible revelation for all to examine. The Christian's book is different! The diamond of Christianity passes the non-contradictory test, when much scope for contradiction was present. Fulfilled Bible prophecy alone compels the conclusion that it is God's infallible word.

By very definition, the Biblical record is permanent and unchanging. It is obtainable and examinable. And it claims to be God's authoritative revelation. Just as the living Word of God, the Lord Jesus, stated 'I am the way, the truth, and the life. No one comes to the Father except through Me'[81] so the written word of God claims that it alone is the revealed expression of His will.[82]

The resurrection and basic Christian teaching

Now see the relevance of the resurrection to the fundamental difference between Christianity and other religions. Salvation is not by good works. It comes when I recognise that I have offended God by my rebellious acts, words, and thoughts. I recognise that I must be judged eternally by a righteous and holy all-knowing God. I am guilty. I stand condemned. But the whole punishment and judgment for my sins fell, from the Father's hand, upon the willing and loving incarnate

Son so that I escape condemnation. I see that the Father accepted the sacrifice of His Son on my behalf by raising Him from the dead. And it is the same power that raised the Son to life that helps me to live a new life. That same power gives victory over the fear of coming, but conquered death. I can look forward to meeting my glorious Lord as my Friend and Saviour at death, or His return.

The supremacy of the gospel

Contrast the poverty of teaching from other religions. No God to love them and become a man—Emmanuel—as a substitute to take their place and punishment. Self-made leaders giving man-made tenets, not the eternal Son who died and rose again. No sense of certainty of forgiveness or eternal life. Their leaders are dead. No comforting Christ in (them) the hope of glory.[83] What have they to look forward to? No conquered tomb or glorious and triumphant return of their leaders.

The light that makes the jewel sparkle!

The resurrection underlines and highlights the gloriously unique truths that the Gospel carries like a brilliant white light shining on gems in a jeweller's window. It reveals the beauty and sparkle of our precious Gospel that says the Father accepted Calvary's substitutionary sacrifice. It displays the trustworthiness of the Saviour because He predicted His own death and resurrection. It emphasises His divine nature. It proclaims that Jesus alone has the right and the awesome responsibility and authority to act in His capacity as eternal Judge. It heralds His victory over death. It gives Christian faith its solid and factual, yet miraculous, content and validity as the truth. It is the explanation why God's power is at work in the Christian when he receives Christ. It guarantees that Jesus will have the last word in history at His coming again, which would have been impossible had He never risen. It also provides the Christian's certainty that a home in heaven is reserved for him!

Opposition reveals the gospel's distinctive nature

It can clearly be seen why there is so much opposition to the Christian's insistence on Christ's resurrection, and the apostolic dogmatism that 'Nor is there salvation in any other, for there is no other name under heaven given among men by which we must be saved.'[84] Peter, in saying this, was addressing the Sanhedrin (religious leaders' council), and was explaining the miraculous healing of the lame man by proclaiming 'by the name of Jesus Christ of Nazareth, whom you crucified, whom God raised from the dead, by Him this man stands here whole.' He declared that salvation was only by faith in the living Lord Jesus

Christ. The resurrection means that only Jesus Christ can meet the real needs of sinful men and women.

Man is fallen

Man-made religion glorifies man's supposed ability to gain God's acceptance. The Gospel of the risen Lord cuts down our pride, insisting that Salvation is of the LORD.[85] Sinful rebellious man does not care for that emphasis!

Sinners can be certain of forgiveness

So the diamond glistens and glitters against the dullness of man-made religious pebbles. God says we cannot save ourselves, but He can: 'by grace you have been saved through faith, and that not of yourselves, it is the gift of God, not of works, lest anyone should boast.' We cannot contribute to our forgiveness, yet we can know the certainty of having eternal life through trusting our risen Shepherd who said of those who came to know Him 'I give them eternal life, and they shall never perish; neither shall anyone snatch them out of My hand.' The resurrection power of Christ motivates and enables those failed sinners who trust Him so that they can say with Paul 'I can do all things through Christ who strengthens me.'[86] All this is because Jesus Christ is the Lord of glory, the eternal co-equal second person of the Trinity, with all the attributes and character of God, and the one who is our 'Emmanuel.' He bore our sins in His own body when He died on the cross, bearing our punishment. He lives today, after His miraculous, historical and physical resurrection.

Living Lord, not dead prophet

We have seen the difference between this God-breathed Gospel that 'Christ Jesus came into the world to save sinners'[87] and man-made religion of whatever type or origin. We have considered that by His rising from that tomb that was sealed, the Lord Jesus Christ also sealed the unique distinctiveness of Christianity's saving message. At the end of his life, Buddha is reported to have said he was still seeking for truth. Mohammed is dead. Confucius has gone. Popes, Archbishops and Pastors are all in the queue of humanity that is moving up and passing on. But Jesus Christ is risen! He is the 'Author and Finisher of our faith.'[88] He is the almighty Creator who put the universe in place. He is the divine Redeemer who gave Himself for our sins and rose triumphantly from the grave. He ascended to His rightful place in heaven. He will return as King of kings and Lord of lords.

Not a religion but a person

So we do not need to assess each religion, nor seek a flimsy nominal unity either outside or within Christian churches. We will not be vague, under the guise of being gracious and enlightened. We can, and do, assert that anyone whose confidence is in the risen Saviour and who believes the Bible to be God's word has absolute truth in their heart and in their hands. We have real unity, though agreeing to disagree on non-essentials. That unity is between all who have received Jesus Christ as Saviour and Lord, irrespective of church or denomination. Our oneness is in Him who died and rose again.

The truth is I cannot save myself, and no man-made concoction of a religion can either. I need a Saviour: the living and eternal Lord Jesus Christ.

Do you know Him?

The resurrection: My Lord and my God

Where do I stand personally?

Honest doubts

We can all identify with Doubting Thomas. In the realm of believing, most of us either have been or are where he has been. Is it possible to identify not only with his doubts but also with his blessing that followed? Happily, God never holds honest doubts against an honest seeker.

Here is the passage in full:

But Thomas, called Didymus, one of the twelve, was not with them when Jesus came. The other disciple therefore said to him, 'We have seen the Lord.' But he said to them, 'Unless I see in His hands the print of the nails, and put my finger into His side, I will not believe.'

And after eight days His disciples were again inside, and Thomas with them. Jesus came, the doors being shut, and stood in the midst, and said, 'Peace to you!' Then He said to Thomas, 'Reach your finger here, and look at my hands; and reach your hand here, and put it into My side. Do not be unbelieving, but believing.' And Thomas answered and said to Him, 'My Lord and my God!'

Jesus said to him, 'Thomas, because you have seen Me, you have believed. Blessed are those who have not seen and yet have believed.'[89]

Eight day delay

Note that it was eight days after appearing to the other disciples that Jesus came to Thomas. Sometimes God allows us to wrestle with our doubts so that we are prepared for His answer. Criticism may give way to questioning, and doubts change to searching. Honest searching always leads us to Christ, who said 'Seek and you will find'.[90]

Honest reservations

Thomas heard the testimony of the disciples and was sceptical. Unless he could see and touch the wounds of the crucified carpenter's son, he would not believe. Today, we seem to live on two extremes—some believe almost anything they are told, whilst others refuse to believe in the face of overwhelmingly convincing evidence. Thomas's stance was not that unreasonable: 'Seeing is believing!' He would believe if ... after all the other disciples claimed they had first-hand evidence!

We should respect the non-Christian who sincerely expresses his reservations. God does not require you to open your mouth and swallow the creed but to be honest about yourself and factually unbiased in your consideration of the Christian message. If that process involves telling disciples of Christ that one is unsure, then so be it. Many Christians have been there! Few of us came easily to a saving faith in Jesus Christ.

In fact, one significant evidence for the resurrection is that Thomas The Doubter, became convinced. The stories of those who seemed to be neutral, sceptical or even enemies of the Gospel having their lives revolutionised when they trusted our risen Saviour is a big plus in favour of the factuality and power of the Gospel.

Subjective and objective
When Christ appeared to Thomas, the others were there. They shared the same personal experience. This blend of fact and experience is convincing. It is the same today. All who turn to Him experience personally the new birth as God the Holy Spirit dwells in their lives. Yet this subjective experience is not the authority upon which we rely. We rely rather on the truth of God's word, the Bible, which has never been found wanting where men have tested it by the facts rather than by their theories. The experience of millions world-wide throughout the ages shows the objective reality that Jesus Christ enters lives and revolutionises them. I am not an odd bod. Millions know Him too!

Closed doors
Jesus showed again His resurrection power and resurrection body. He appeared to His disciples on the other side of a closed door. Closed doors were no problem! This action confirmed the disciples' faith. What about the 'closed doors' of our prejudices? He often passes through them. Some thought they would never be converted. Real or imaginary doubt or lack of understanding seemed to slam the doors firmly shut. Yet Christ answers that seemingly feeble prayer 'Lord, I believe; help my unbelief.'[91] He passes through our closed doors to show us our sin and need, and the answer in Himself, His death and resurrection.

Peace
The Lord Jesus' opening salutation was 'Peace to you!' This had also been his earlier message to the group of disillusioned believers. It is repeated for Thomas. Our personal God longs to give His peace to the individual sinner. Our sin

makes us at enmity with God. It robs us of tranquillity within, through our guilty conscience and fear of death. We are not ready to die, but have no real peace in living. Sin prevents us from living in harmony with our fellow men. Christ comes to us. He has taken the righteous punishment from a holy God against our sins on the cross. Whilst smitten by God and afflicted 92 there, an eternity of hell's judgment was contracted into three hours and poured out in concentrated wrath upon Him. He died. He rose from the dead! As we turn to Him in repentance, He enters our lives through the Holy Spirit. He gives us 'the peace of God which surpasses all understanding'93 as we own His lordship in our lives. He changes our attitudes to others too, and motivates us to go to others with the same message of the living Prince of peace! In a world of turmoil and uncertainty, the Lord Jesus Christ offers peace.

Personal assurance

Jesus took Thomas at his word! He gave him the opportunity to both see and feel His wounds. How wonderfully long-suffering is our Self-revealing God! What lengths He has gone to in order to reveal Himself to us through the living Word, the Lord Jesus, and the written word, the Bible. Both are open to thorough, exhaustive and critical examination.

But, in addition to this, He sometimes steps outside the ample means of grace He has provided, hearing our poor expressions of unbelief and gives us further personal assurances of His existence and love for us. Our faith and peace would be stronger, and more quickly assured, if we would simply take Him at His word. Yet, although we have no promise to claim and therefore cannot count upon it, He often gives us a specific personal answer to some specific irrational doubt. Just as there is no record of Thomas ever touching those wounds, however, so we begin to realise the folly of our unbelief when we come to know the risen Saviour. The only assurance we need is found when we trust Him.

Response

The response of Thomas is a classic pattern for any who would come to know the Lord—'My Lord and my God!' It says it all. It was personal. He said, 'my Lord', 'my God'. It was worshipful. He saw that the Man of Calvary was also the Lord God of eternity. It was submissive. He owned Jesus as his Lord.

Jesus told Thomas: 'Thomas, because you have seen Me, you have believed. Blessed are those who have not seen and yet have believed.' We can know that same blessing by following the response that Thomas made. Like him, I can look back to the historic darkness of Calvary when Jesus bore my sins in His own body on the tree94 as He was judged in my place. Like him, I can meet the risen Lord who conquered sin and death!

Personal, worshipful, submissive

My response must be personal. I am a guilty sinner under condemnation. The penitent publican's personal prayer must be mine: 'God be merciful to me a sinner.'[95]

My response must be worshipful. I am coming to the one true God, the holy, almighty, and majestic Lord of all. People feel nervous when they go to Buckingham Palace to collect their honours. How much more should I tremble at the thought of meeting the Eternal One. But for the righteousness, death and resurrection of my living Advocate and Friend I would be consumed on contact. Never forget that my God is holy. No-one can approach Him for forgiveness unless willing to leave their sins behind and yield to Him.

My response must be submissive. Repentance means that I vacate the throne of my own life. It is for the King of glory. He must rule, not only in principle, but as evidenced by daily obedience as I live in His power and grace.

Respond now!

Thomas also responded immediately. Do you know Jesus Christ as your Saviour from sin, death, and hell?

Life is short. Death is sure. Eternity is long. And God is too great, too loving, and too sovereign for me to delay. God's time for getting right is always 'now.' Tomorrow may not belong to me. If it does, I may not be as open again to turn to Him. I may even go on and harden my heart so that God ceases to plead with me. If my house is on fire, I escape as soon as I can. I do not hang around.

And what an assured welcome the moment I turn to Him, 'for whoever calls on the name of the LORD shall be saved'.[96] Call on Him. Tell Him your doubts. Bring them with you so He can deal with them. But come also

with your sins, confessing and forsaking them, and ask Him to forgive you and enter your life as your living Saviour and Lord. Then express to Him, and others, your gratitude that you can know and say, 'He is my Lord and my God!'

The test of resurrection reality

Over the years since Christ's resurrection it has not been hard to tell when someone has come to know the risen Lord. Their life changes! They rejoice that they know Christ. They spend time daily reading His word, the Bible. They pray every day, and even through the day (though no-one around may know), knowing their prayers do not just hit the ceiling. They keep Sunday as the Lord's Day, resisting the temptation to do everyday work or to follow the world in its mad pursuit of passing pleasures on His special day. They consecrate the day to Him and attending a church faithfully where the Bible is taught and the Lord is honoured. During the week they will seek the fellowship of other Christians both in meetings, large or small, and in meaningful open fellowship with individual Christian friends. And in the steps of the apostles and of the early church, they not only live a new life but also witness boldly, and wisely, to all around.

When you yield to the Lord Jesus, the same change of appetite and priority will become yours. The evidence of conversion is a desire to get to know Him better and to make Him better known. It is not always easy. There are times when you will especially need God's strength, against the temptation to give in, give up, or compromise here and there. But blessing rests in putting the risen Lord first in your life.

Witnessing for Christ

Friends and acquaintances will notice the difference! Be prayerful, be wise, be gracious—but do be faithful in sharing with them, as the opportunity presents itself, what Christ has done for you. I know some believers who ask God to let them witness to at least one person a day by what they say, and how they live. It is an honouring and exacting goal, but God can give grace to meet it. Certainly it follows the lead of those who first proclaimed, with great results, the Gospel of Christ crucified and risen from the dead. For them it brought opposition, and even persecution. There may be a cost for you too, but we must share our urgent message of God's love with lost men and women.

In the early church the authorities and religious leaders were 'greatly disturbed that they taught the people and preached in Jesus the resurrection from the dead'.[97] After the apostles had used their apostolic power to heal a man in the name of Jesus, they told their interrogators 'let it be known to you all, and to all the people of Israel, that by the name of Jesus Christ of Nazareth, whom you crucified, whom God raised from the dead, by Him this man stands here before you whole'. 'Being warned by them not to speak at all nor teach in the name of Jesus they continued, and with great power the apostles gave witness to the resurrection of the Lord Jesus. And great grace was upon them all.'

Grace to you

God gave them grace to tell all they could that Christ had died for their sins and risen again. He will give you that same grace as you determine to share your Lord each day with others! Do not worry about opposition, as long as you are living wisely and witnessing graciously for Him.

Your Lord and your God has a task for you to do for Him! Be like Thomas, and pass from scepticism, through salvation to service for the risen Saviour who loves you!

The resurrection: keep looking up!

Seeking a Heavenly lifestyle for holy living.

'After you get what you want, you don't want it'

Most people seek for better things because they have not yet found anything that satisfies or lasts. Why does a millionaire turn to drugs? Why does a man with a beautiful wife pursue an alley cat lifestyle? Why does a world celebrity turn to homosexuality? Why does a successful businessman opt out for the life style of a recluse?

Because what they have does not satisfy them. Marilyn Monroe, the icon sex star of her era, crooned 'After you get what you want, you don't want it.' She was right, and her sad life and tragic death in mysterious circumstances, underlined that the world cannot satisfy the deepest needs and longings of the human heart.

Most people seek because they have not found.

After you come to Christ you want to know Him better

But Biblical Christianity, as in all other things, is completely different. The Christian seeks because he has found. He finds that God's grace and mercy in Christ have led him to such a fruitful valley of new resurrection life that he wants to return there often. Despite the constant battle with the coldness and hardness of his sinful heart, he nevertheless has tasted that new fruit, feasted his eyes on that previously unimagined beauty, and sensed the fragrance of that valley which he never knew existed before He came to Christ. He has drunk the clean and refreshing waters flowing from the pure life-giving Spring. Although assailed by the world, the flesh and the devil, he knows now that 'none but Christ can satisfy' and so he comes back again and again to the true Fountain of life.

In short, each person who has come to know Christ will want to know Him better. He or she loves the One who 'loved me and gave Himself for me'[98] and will want to be with the Lover of his or her soul. That Christian will seek His presence and what pleases Him.

The Bible reflects this motivation in the first four verses of the third chapter of Paul's letter to the Colossians:

If then you were raised with Christ, seek those things which are above, where Christ is sitting at the right hand of God. Set your mind on things above, not on things on the earth, For you died and your life is hidden with Christ in God. When Christ, who is our life appears, then you will appear with Him in glory.

The passage goes on to give very practical advice as to how the Christian should, and should not, live in the light of the truths springing from being raised with Christ. We need to give heed to its teaching. The resurrection of Christ must not stay only in the vaults of our theological orthodoxy, but be translated into holy Christian living on a daily basis.

Conversion starts with seeking

It is only when a man turns from his sins and seeks Christ that he is forgiven.

He cannot become a Christian just by making a superficial decision, or receiving Christ merely in order to gain peace, joy, love, power or satisfaction. True, having repented and trusted the Lord, he will have 'peace with God',[99] 'joy inexpressible and full of glory'[100] and the power of the Holy Spirit in his life. Also he will know a deep sense of satisfaction because he has come into living fellowship with his Maker, and he was made for that. But his coming to Christ was because he was repentantly seeking God's forgiveness. He had to come wholeheartedly—or not at all— for God has said 'you will seek Me and find Me when you search for Me with all your heart.'[101] Jesus said 'seek, and you will find'.[102] Seeking implies seriousness and a real concern to find.

Seeking then becomes a Christian's lifestyle

Seeking is not only vital in a sinner's coming to Christ. Like repentance itself, it then becomes the necessary lifestyle of a truly born again Christian. The Bible indicates many areas of life in which a follower of Christ has to pursue that same earnest desire to seek, as when he first came to faith in his crucified and risen Lord.

It is only through the God-given desire after conversion, that we have any inclination or determination to seek the things that God values. Without it we would please ourselves. Yet when we seek what pleases Him, we are greatly blessed though our seeking and finding are partial. A person in love can find an amazing interest in what his loved one likes, even though he would have preferred to watch paint dry rather than engage in those things before his new relationship! So when we come to know and love Christ, we want to please Him and to seek and love the things that He loves. In fact, that is a good test of whether we have really come to know Him, and that is what Colossians 3 verse 1 underlines: '*If* then you were raised with Christ, *seek those things* which are above' (my emphasis).

The background—resurrection and pre-eminence

The book of Colossians is what every Christian should be: *Christ-centred*. Chapter 1, verses 17 and 18 summarise the importance of His resurrection and His absolute sovereignty. The chapter shows His pre-eminence in His deity, His eternal pre-existence, His position as Creator, His headship of the church, and in His resurrection.

And He is *before all things*, and in Him all things consist. And He is the *head of the body, the church*, who is the beginning, *the firstborn from the dead*, that in all things *He may have the pre-eminence*. (My emphases).

Resurrected Christ = risen Christians!

Chapter two encourages the Christians not to be taken in by those who would deny or distort those eternal truths. Verses 11 to 17 state that those trusting Christ 'also were raised with Him through faith in the working of God, Who raised Him from the dead'. That is followed by two reminders. First, they had been 'dead in (their) trespasses and the uncircumcision of (their) flesh'. Second, 'He has made (them) alive together with Him, having forgiven (them) all trespasses'.

They had been dead under sin. Christ had died for their sins and taken the penalty for their sins that they deserved. He had risen again from the dead, and so they had been made alive by and in Him, the risen Lord of the universe and of the church. They had been forgiven completely and so possessed new life in Him.

The second chapter goes on to warn them against getting entangled in the legalistic requirements of men. This is because they had died in Christ and had received life on a new plane in their risen Lord. Man-made rules could neither change that death, nor produce or remove that life, and must not contaminate their new life which came solely by faith in the living Lord, and not by works that they had done.

But a risen life in Christ did impose upon them, and still does upon us, some obligations and duties!

The ruthless logic of the risen life

Some preachers unwisely repeat that we can be 'too Heavenly-minded to be of any earthly use'. Undiscerning members of congregations may laugh at the misleading comment. It is easier to criticise and ridicule Heavenly-mindedness than it is to live it. Perhaps that is why we joke about it.

The truth, demonstrated by a 'great cloud of witnesses', both Biblical and historical, is the reverse. In order to be of increasing use to God on earth, we need to be more, not less, Heavenly-minded. It is essential, therefore, that we should seek 'things — above' and have our minds 'set' on them. There is a rationale of resurrection to be outworked in the area of personal holiness. There is ruthless logic about the risen life. Because Jesus died your death for you, He now lives in you. You have a new resurrection life. He has raised you to be with Him spiritually now: that is what conversion is. That will be your long-term lifestyle in Heaven. In fact, it *is now* your long-term lifestyle. *Live it!*

Be consistent

Let us follow that through. Sin is basically living our lives our way, and not God's way. It involves selfishly following our readily accepted preferences as well as obvious sins. How can we live like that if we are grateful that Jesus died the death we deserve, for us? How can we celebrate our new life by living as if we were in the old one and following its preferences and rebellion? How can we insult Him by thanking Him for dying for us and then choosing the very lifestyle that caused Him to die?

If we regard ourselves as dead to sin, by taking up our cross (an instrument of execution) daily and following Him, how can we decide to live as we want? Dead men do not have preferences! We are to 'reckon' ourselves as 'dead to sin'.[103]

Christ has become our Saviour and Lord! He has given us eternal life now that will expand into eternity. We will never feel at home scratching around the dustbins of our previous lives! Is it more consistent to eat rancid left- over scraps, thrown out by a fast food restaurant, when we could be dining as guests at a banquet? We have a life in 'resurrection city': we must not camp in the graveyard of our past lost lives. We are to 'reckon' ourselves as 'alive to God in Christ Jesus our Lord'.[104]

A new nature is marked by new priorities, new standards, a new appetite, and new joys. If you have been raised with Christ, these can only be found in a resurrection lifestyle.

If you rejoice that you will be in Heaven with Christ forever, you know that there is no better place to be. Then why not enjoy as much of that down here as you can? How can you prize that for eternity, but scorn it for your little time on earth? In fact, sanctification's goal is to close that gap! We will all notice a tremendous change between Heaven and earth, but we can prepare for it as much as possible now. How? By seeking 'those things which are above'. It will bring more of Heaven to our souls down here.

Where to seek and what to seek?

Where are the things we are to seek? They are 'above'. They are where Christ is 'even at the right hand of God.'[105] They are therefore in glory. That is where Jesus is and where, one day, we will be with Him 'and we shall be like Him'.[106]

Since we know *where* the things we must seek are located, we can learn easily *what* they are. The book of Revelation draws back the curtain of eternity and previews glory for us. Chapters 4 and 5 let us look through a 'door standing open in Heaven' and chapters 21 and 22 reveal the character of God's eternal dwelling, as the New Jerusalem descends from Heaven to earth. What follows below is based on those four chapters but is not a verse by verse analysis. Please read those chapters to have a panoramic view of that great and eternal state of blessing.

Four important principles

There are, at least, four important principles operating in glory. These are 'things above' that we should seek to have in focus, whilst journeying towards our eternal home. Their glorious fulfilment will await us when we get there! Those principles are the centrality of Christ, the reality of eternity, the desire for holiness, and the importance of fellowship. If we are 'risen with Christ', these will form important priorities in our spiritual life style.

The centrality of Christ

In Heaven, the Lord Jesus Christ is the object of *praise*. Be it as the Lamb in the midst of the throne, or as the temple of New Jerusalem, or as the very light of Heaven obviating the need for the sun, Jesus is central. He must be the centre of our praise, too. Many hymns focus too much on the sentiments of the worshipper rather than on the supremacy of the once slain, now risen and ascended, Lamb of God. We must focus on Him in our worship, and not on our worship of Him.

Similarly in *presenting the gospel* we must, with Paul, determine 'not to know anything among you except Jesus Christ and Him crucified'.[107] The gospel is not primarily defined by its results in our life—wonderful as they are—but by the fact that God in Christ bore our sins and their punishment on the cross and rose again from the dead. We are saved only when we come to *Him* in repentance and faith, remembering that He clearly stated that 'No one comes to the Father except through Me'.

Our *daily walk* should also centre upon Christ. 'As you have therefore received Christ Jesus the Lord, so walk *in Him*' says the Bible.[108] We do not grow as Christians through a mere mechanics of holiness. To spend a set time in daily devotions and to read highly recommended 'sound' books is good, but not enough. We must get close to Christ in order to progress. Those valuable and essential daily means of grace are, after all, only 'means'. We must surrender daily to our risen Master, and get to know Him better.

Seeking the 'things above' means keeping our risen Lord Jesus in the centre of our praise, our preaching and our personal walk. He must be Lord of these three areas.

The reality of eternity

The next thing to seek is an attitude that recognises that only eternal things are real and lasting. Everything about those four chapters in Revelation shouts 'Eternity!' at us. The whole scene is a glorious climax to the amazing and mind-boggling events in the world. It emphasises not only the preeminence, but also the eternal permanence of God Almighty and the Lamb and the ongoing worship due to Deity alone. The words 'forever and ever' are written across every scene and every thought. Eternity *is* real and, by definition, will continue so to be. Only time and this world are passing. If we have received eternal life through faith in the slain, risen, ascended, and reigning Lamb, then we too must have 'eternity' superimposed on everything we see. This will touch how we live, serve, spend our time and money, seek lost men and women, value other believers, and seek to honour and worship Him. All these, and much more, follow our seeking to build on the reality of eternity. A firm once gave me a pair of sunglasses (or 'shades' if you prefer!) as an advertising promotion. Because the firm's name was printed on one lens, it was superimposed on everything I saw. We should have 'eternity' printed across our Christian vision, so that we see and evaluate everything in its light and certainty. We would live differently if that were so.

The desire for holiness

The third theme from the preview of glory given by these chapters is holiness. The Lord God Almighty is referred to as 'Holy, Holy, Holy' and Revelation chapter 4 emphasises the great gulf between our three times holy God and ourselves. An approach seems impossible until the Lamb appears in the next chapter as our Redeemer. And it is only because He has 'redeemed us to God by [His] blood' that we can approach God.

In the last two chapters of the Bible we see that no entry into New Jerusalem is allowed to do 'anything that defiles, or causes an abomination or a lie'. The word 'holy' does not appear in chapter 21, but the fact of absolute holiness is demonstrated by this separation from all sin, even sin that 'only' causes a lie! In chapter 22, not only does the word itself recur but the purity of the 'river of water of life, clear as crystal' underlines that we are looking at 'the holy city'. That holiness causes the exclusion of 'dogs and sorcerers and sexually immoral and murderers and idolaters, and whoever loves and practises a lie'.

Holiness provides the essential environment for God's glorious Heaven. It is the very essence of the spiritual air that is breathed. 'Pursue holiness, without which no-one will see the Lord'[109] is a clear requirement of God's word.

Holiness is the entrance qualification for entry into Heaven, attributed to the Christian solely on the grounds of His Saviour's holy and spotless life. It is also a description of the only way to appreciate and rejoice in God's immediate presence. The very thought of worldly attitudes, words, actions, music and entertainments in Heaven is untenable. To say that the things we seek above include holiness is a point almost too obvious to make.

Worldliness is illogical and unscriptural

It is illogical for a Christian to ignore holiness, but to engage actively in worldliness. Such a love for the world is often expressed in our choice of music, TV or videos, entertainment, lifestyle, humour, fashion, close friendships, reading material, ambition, thinking, philosophy and standards. It is frequently displayed by our attitudes towards sex and money. The command is clear. 'Seek those things which are above'. So much that we accept unflinchingly today was once clearly out of bounds for followers of the risen Christ. Things now often generally accepted by Christians belong to the mentality of the broad way that leads to destruction. People fully given to those things will spend eternity apart from God. How, therefore, can we have fellowship with them in those things now? If we are really little, or no different from lost and condemned humanity, how can we be sure that we have been truly 'born again' and that our citizenship is in Heaven and not in Hell?

If that distinctive holiness we see 'above' is missing from our lives below, how can we claim to be God's ambassadors to a hostile world? Words are cheap. A holy lifestyle costs and counts. Do we have it? Are we part of it? Are we really serious about setting our 'mind on things above, not on things on the earth'? If the absence of seeking Christ's glory now puts into question whether we have been 'raised with Christ', how do we know that He has worked in us, in real saving and sanctifying grace, so that we shall enjoy glory with Him finally?

We shall always be assailed by the world, the flesh and the devil. Even Jesus was sorely tempted, and so shall we be. At times we will feel like a battlefield— and we will be! John Newton wrote: 'What opposites I feel within: the rule of grace, the power of sin.'

We should expect our desires for holiness to be bombarded by all kinds of enemy action, but if there is no desire to be holy, how can the Holy Spirit, the Spirit of holiness, be active in my life?

The importance of fellowship

A young member of the United Beach Missions team at Llandudno, North Wales, went to the holiday-makers' service, run by the local evangelical church. He had the privilege of sitting under the ministry of Horace Jones, its pastor. At the end of the service he approached the pastor to say 'Goodbye', and overheard a brief conversation, between a grateful holidaymaker and the pastor, that taught that young man a lot about fellowship.

'Thank you for your fellowship, Mr Jones' said the holidaymaker.
'Oh', replied the godly little Welshman in a soft tone, and with a twinkle in his eye, 'please don't thank me. You brought it with you!'

What fellowship is not
Fellowship is not a mere meeting, though it should exist in every Christian meeting. It is not friendship, though it is the ideal seed-bed in which helpful friendships will grow. It does not consist of feelings alone, though can encourage godly emotions and lead to great peace, joy and gratitude. Fellowship is not something you go to: it is an attitude you have, and take with you. It literally means 'sharing'. It comes from knowing Christ and being like-minded with others who know Him.

What fellowship 'above' is like
All who have benefited from our Lord's death and resurrection will one day share the fellowship above, described in the four chosen chapters of Revelation. Meanwhile, we should seek that kind of fellowship here on earth. The three other great principles to seek above provide the seed bed in and from which Christian fellowship can grow and flourish. Dilute the emphasis on the Lord Jesus and our fellowship becomes humanistic, even though dressed in spiritual phrases. Ignore eternity by limiting our thinking to the present, and the spiritual value of fellowship with others will evaporate. Allow a worldly attitude and mind-set amongst those having fellowship and any spiritual relationship is relegated to mere comradeship that one could find in any group of people who cannot relate to each other spiritually.

In the chapters under consideration we can see some characteristics of that higher fellowship:

1. It includes saved people from many different backgrounds—yet they are one;

2. It involves all in the same purpose—there is single-mindedness, no personal agendas to follow, and complete transparency with each other reflecting an open relationship with God;

3. It majors on the great truths of God—no error enters and no peripheral divisions spoil it—and thus it flourishes in an atmosphere of true worship and submission;

4. It is marked by God's Spirit, and thus by order and meaning that does not dampen godly enthusiasm;

5. It honours God—He is more important than anyone else;

6. It includes thankfulness—no grumbling, gossiping or groaning is heard;

7. It recognises eldership—but the elders themselves were examples in humility, zeal and sacrifice.

There are millions of worshippers in Heaven from all over. Some are notable celebrities and high-powered beings. But it is not the huge numbers, or the great gifts of any of those people that predominates. The presence and fact of the triune God form the centre of that ordered and enthusiastic fellowship, expressed in thankful and reverent rejoicing, worship, and submission.

True fellowship is not merely the immediate 'buzz' of the positive peer group, or the feeling that we are being carried along by the majority. This oneness comes from knowing and loving the Lord Jesus Christ and leads us to an openness with God and with each other. Of course, there will be times of emotion, individually and together, as we concentrate on who the living Lord Jesus is and what He has done for us. But that is a result of trusting and surrendering our lives to Him.

We must seek this to encourage the quality of fellowship by our prayers and actions. It will go hand in hand with the other three priorities. In fact each priority, prayerfully sought, will help us to seek the others.

How do we seek these things?

But how do we, who have entered in to the blessings of trusting the risen Lord, seek those four 'things which are above'? How do we apply those principles, here on earth? And how do we keep on seeking them? That is the sense of the verse—'keep seeking the things above' (NASB). This is a daily battle to be fought. It is a life quest to be achieved bit by bit each day. We must pray and seek the centrality of Christ, the reality of eternity, a desire for holiness, and real spiritual fellowship. And we must apply those priorities to our lives in the resurrection power of our Lord Jesus.

Achieving this is very practical and very challenging. We see how to do that, in God's strength, in Colossians chapter 3, verse 1 to chapter 4 verse 5. You could call the passage 'Ten pointers to successful seeking'.

Ten pointers to successful seeking

We will list the pointers and then look at some of the practical outworking. If we are seeking sincerely, our lives will change.

1. Focus on Christ, and set your mind Heavenwards

We focus on Christ and make a deliberate choice to set our minds on Heavenly eternal things, rather than temporary worldly things. (Chapter 3 verses 1–2) I cannot be a serious seeker of spiritual things unless I make much of my Saviour and refuse to bow at the shrines of worldly values and pleasures.

2. Dead but still dying
We remember that we 'have died', and that now God sees us as 'hidden with Christ in God'. (Chapter 3, verse 2) That is our happy position in Christ. Our standing is clear. But often our state is different, and we must apply in practice what we know in principle, namely that we have died. We must now put to death anything inconsistent with our walk with the Lord of resurrection. (Chapter 3 verses 5 and 6)

3. His glorious coming and my glorious future
We encourage ourselves by reflecting on His second coming, and the eternal glory we will share with Him. (Chapter 3 verse 4) If we have our minds fixed on the real and eternal future, we will begin to live out a life style that is consistent with it.

4. We 'put off' and we 'put on'
We put off the filthy rags that defiled and characterised our old life, and put on the new garments of God's elect and beloved people. (Chapter 3 verses 8 to 14) This is ongoing repentance in action.

5. The rule of God's peace
We let God's peace rule our hearts. (Chapter 3 verse 15) This can only be when the risen Prince of Peace has Lordship of our lives, and when we constantly seek to submit to Him. Unless our biblically informed and spiritually renewed conscience can act in peace, because we have determined to please God in what we do, we do not move on in any action or course of conduct.

6. God's word generously treasured within
We let Christ's word dwell richly in us (Chapter 3 verse 16). No day should go by without spending quality time in His word, and no week should go by without listening to His word on the Lord's Day and at other times of fellowship and Bible study.

7. Realising His presence in every situation and being pro-actively thankful
We do everything in His name and thank Him whilst we do it (Chapter 3 verses 17). The resurrected Lord, who will never forsake us, wants us to realise His presence throughout the day, in mundane and exceptional circumstances alike. He delights when 'in everything [we] give thanks, for this is the will of God for [us]'.[110]

8. Do it!
We then apply all that to our station and circumstances in life (Chapter 3, verse 18 to Chapter 4 verse 1). More of this later in the chapter.

9. Never stop praying

We continue praying, and especially for the proclaiming of the 'mystery of Christ'. (Chapter 4 verse 2). We can only continue what we have started already! We must cultivate a daily spirit of prayer by starting each day with God in meaningful communion with Him. We will be zealous to pray with our churches and God's people during the week. We will pray for the furtherance of the gospel, that the 'word of the Lord may run *swiftly* and be glorified',[111] and plead for help for God's servants at home and abroad, and for lost souls to be saved.

10. Wise walk and careful talk

We walk wisely and talk carefully. (Chapter 4 verses 5 and 6). The wisdom we need is available on sincere demand from God.[112] The same letter of James focuses strongly on the need for control of the tongue.[113] If we are serious about seeking 'those things above', we will grow in wisdom. This will affect noticeably both what we say and what we refrain from saying.

Practical outworking

The Bible mixes and blends doctrinal and spiritual truth with practical application. This is often done in the doctrinal or spiritual passage itself. The same is true of chapters 3 and 4 of Colossians, as indicated in the previous paragraph.

However, there are particularly practical emphases that the Holy Spirit has underlined in those chapters. Those knowing the living Christ and the benefits of His resurrection, must translate their Heavenly seeking into very down to earth behaviour. That seeking must make a real difference in living. This chapter concludes by examining briefly each of the four areas concerned.

Those areas are control of temper, control of the tongue, relationships with fellow Christians, and interaction in everyday life with those with whom we have a special relationship.

Control of temper

Colossians 3, verse 8, gives a list of sinful attitudes and actions and says that we must 'put off *all* these things'. I have emphasised the word 'all', because this is not like a multiple choice examination paper where you can select which sins to get rid off. They *all* have to be put off. It is not enough to claim a weak personality, or extreme provocation. God says the man or woman with the resurrection life of Christ within, must put off them *all*.

Anger, wrath, and malice head up the list. That in itself is worthy of note since, however they may be later expressed, they all are essentially inward things. Our actions show what is the true state of our heart. Jesus taught this clearly, as we see from Mark 7 verses 21 to 27:

And He said, 'What comes out of a man, that defiles a man. For from within, out of the heart of men, proceed evil thoughts, adulteries, fornications, murders, thefts, covetousness, wickedness, deceit, lewdness, an evil eye, blasphemy, pride, foolishness. All these evil things come from within and defile a man.'

Have you noticed that the sins of the tongue follow next in the list? The mouth is to the heart, what an amplifier is to a CD player. Our words reveal what is the true state of our heart.

The often-quoted words are, indeed, very true: '*the heart of the problem is the problem of the heart.*' God's advice to every child of His, is 'My son [or daughter, of course] give me your heart'.[114] He knows that we should 'Keep [our] heart with all diligence, For out of it *spring* the issues of life'.[115]

That is why we need an open, honest, continual, repentant attitude towards God, bolstered by the dual confidence that 'the blood of Jesus Christ His Son cleanses us from all sin'[116] and 'God gives grace to the humble'.[117] Only by constant transparent honesty before God can we know His continual cleansing that keeps us in fellowship with Him, and His Spirit's prompting that can keep us from sin.

Practically, when we feel like losing our tempers, or building up a wrathful attitude to someone, or even acting in malice to 'get even with' (or even get ahead of) others, we need to run to the throne of grace and cry 'Help, LORD!'[118] We need to remind ourselves that if we are willing to reckon ourselves as dead to the sin within and to be constantly changed within, we have the full resurrection power of Christ to enable that to take place. Self-control is part of the fruit of the Spirit, and it is only in this way that we can ask the Holy Spirit to control us, fill us and help us.

Control of the tongue

We have seen that walking in God's wisdom helps us to control the use of our tongues. God gives grace to those who are humble enough to ask for His wisdom and who know that they have no real wisdom of their own. That grace not only changes our hearts and minds, but determines how and when we speak. But chapter 3, verse 8 to 10, is even more specific. It teaches that those of us trusting the risen Lord must put off, not only anger, wrath and malice, but also blasphemy, filthy language, and lying.

The battle sometimes rages within our hearts in the realm of controlling our temper and our reactions. When God is really given control of our lips, we avoid the trouble that we often cause.

People would not be hurt by our words and we would not spoil our testimony to non-Christians as we may do too often. Our testimony is like a big window pane through which others can observe God's grace and truth in action in our lives. It can take a long time to put that window in place and we spend time regularly keeping it clean. But, alas, it can be broken in a second by ungodly, idle, selfish, unkind, malicious, or untrue words.

Not a means of evangelism, but—!

Happily for us, God always forgives us when we are truly repentant and confess our sins to Him. He can even take our bad verbal testimony and turn it into good! It is amazing what God's grace accomplishes when we go humbly to a person we have wronged, admit we are to blame, and ask his or her forgiveness. That is not a means of evangelism or fellowship we should plan on adopting! Nevertheless, it is comforting to hear of those who were impressed by a Christian's readiness to admit wrong and accept responsibility and blame.

The list of the sins of the tongue starts with 'blasphemy'. We can dishonour God's name by singing hymns or choruses that are not true. They may be biblically in error, or claim an attitude we do not possess or an experience of God that we do not have. Also we can make superficial promises to Him, with musical accompaniment, that we would never dare to pray to Him on our own, or with others. It is not only the vile language of the pub or the intellectually couched blasphemy of the university senior

common room that offends Him. He expects His own people to differ from the 'wicked' who say 'our lips are our own'.[119]

Isaiah said that he was 'undone' because he was 'a man of unclean lips' who dwelt 'in the midst of a people of unclean lips'.[120] He appreciated the need to put off 'filthy language out of your mouth'. Too many Christians are careless, or rebellious, in the choice of their vocabulary and in using words they do not understand, which are often substitutes for unclean or swear words. Our battle for pure speech is not helped by certain programmes or people on television, video or radio. We can adopt poor or bad language so easily by osmosis, and not be affronted by sin as we ought to be. That is why we should avoid certain programmes and films, and move away from those peddling filthy jokes, whenever it is in our power so to do.

One wonders what problem in the Colossians caused the command; 'Do not lie one to another.' Any form of lying, for any reason, does not befit one who has come to God by the One who said 'I am the way, *the truth*, and the life',[121] or who accepts His words that God's 'word is truth'.[122] The third Person of the Trinity is the 'Holy Spirit of truth,'[123] and those indwelt by

Him should not grieve Him by untruths. 'Nothing that causes a lie' shall enter Heaven,[124] and we should watch our conversation to ensure we reject anything untrue.

Relationships with fellow Christians

Colossians 3 verses 12 to 17, guides us in our relationships with fellow Christians. See what mutual blessings flow between members of the Christian family, as God grants us the Heavenly mind set to help us 'put on' these things in prayer:

tender mercies, kindness, humility, meekness, longsuffering, bearing with one another, and forgiving one another—But above all these things put on love, which is the bond of perfection

In every relationship, forgiveness predominates where Christians seek to translate 'those things above' into daily living. Remember that the result of the victorious battle at Calvary, and the thrilling conquest of the empty tomb by our ever-living High Priest, is that 'Christ forgave you'. Without that we could have no relationship with God. We must thus extend that forgiveness to others as we live for Him below. This we must do until that time when we no longer need to 'seek those things which are above', because we will be with Him in Heaven itself.

Love needed

We need to be so taken up with the only Person who can impart these qualities to us, that we exhibit them increasingly to each other. The history of the universal church, and many local churches too, would be very different if Christians were more earnest in seeking what pleased God. It would have been reflected in the way we treated one another. The key, Paul says, is 'love'. That love surpasses emotional attachment, or an admiration for someone's qualities. It is God-given, and so can be prayed for and worked on with His help. It means seeking the highest good of others at personal cost to ourselves. Jesus always sought the highest good of others, and He is our pattern.

If godly love in inter-Christian relationships was the sole thermometer of our spirituality and love for Christ, how warm would our love be right now?

Interaction within special relationships

We all have special relationships as well as normal relationships with people at large, or our fellowship relationship with other Christians. In Colossians chapter 3, verse 18, to chapter 4, verse 1, we meet wives and husbands, children and parents, and servants and masters. These teach important lessons for today about how to live with our wife or husband, how to bring up children and be brought up by parents, and how to handle the employment situation which is a quasi master-servant relationship. Our media presents each of these arenas as violent gladiatorial struggles. Conflict and breakdown of relationships is the norm. Happy and settled marriages are increasingly rare. Often, neither parents nor children can handle the simplest of conflicts that inevitably arise. The workplace is a minefield of legislation to seek to protect rights and regulate conduct. The sinister hand of man's sinfulness is patently pulling the strings that the evil one himself does not manipulate directly, through a hostile world system.

It is into this arena of strife and spiritual death that the Christian enters with the claim 'it is no longer I who live, but Christ lives in me.'[125] If the light of the risen Christ is to shine in that darkness, Christian conduct has to be distinctively different. But how can this be achieved?

Husbands and wives

In the marriage relationship, the submission of the wife to her own husband, 'as is fitting in the Lord', is reciprocally matched by the husband's all prevailing love for his wife, that rules out bitterness of any kind. That can only be consistently achieved, in this world of pressure and blame, when our minds are being renewed daily by God. In turn, that can only occur when we seek those things which are above, and reflect them in how we live individually and together.

Children and parents

Christian children are not too young to be encouraged to seek those Heavenly values. If they are centred on the risen Christ, they will want to be 'well pleasing to the Lord' and will gladly obey their parents 'in all things'. Fathers have the responsibility for family discipline and so are mentioned in verse 21. Because they have renewed minds, consistent with following their risen Lord, they will be careful to encourage their offspring. Their earnest desire to avoid discouraging them will prevent undue provocation of their children. When they do fail—and which of us has not?—they will humbly ask forgiveness from their own children. Such consistent humility cannot come from a worldly attitude to living, and sets a wonderful example for all members of the family to follow.

Employees and employers

Like the Colossian bondservants, employees who look each day to eternal realities to fashion their lives, will have sincere God-fearing hearts. Consequently they will know that 'The eyes of the Lord are in every place, keeping watch on the evil and the good'[126] and will not work simply to catch the eyes of their seniors. They know they are already seen by their higher Master. They will want to please Him. Hearty fulfillment of duty will be their expression of serving the resurrected 'Lord Christ'. The thought of pilfering time, materials or equipment would be dealt with as Satan's temptation to be resisted, or to be repented of if it ever happened. Their concern will be to give, not to get. Their concern will be to use the money they have honestly earned to glorify God, extend His kingdom, and bless the less privileged.

Employers will behave justly and fairly to their employees, if they have their eye on their Master, the risen Lord of glory. Not only should ultimate accountability determine this. Gratitude towards the One who died and rose again to save them demands it.

God expects us, according to chapter 4, verses 5 and 6, to be especially aware of the outsider in the wise way we must walk. Time is not to be wasted—neither our time nor employer's time. God wants to be able to use our words for Him, and enable us to answer non-Christians in a way that will bless them and honour Him. Again, that calls for an ongoing spiritual life of discipleship and for a focus on those things that really matter.

Spiritual battles cannot be won by non-spiritual means—including the battle to win our employers and fellow workers.

And finally—

Those with the risen Christ enthroned as Lord, will seek a lifestyle for Him on earth that reflects eternal realities above. They will be marked out as different from others. This seeking is continual and daily, involving repentance and faith. They will put off those things that offend God and put on the things He loves. If they are 'risen with Christ' this will follow. If it does not follow, they need to question their claim to be Christians and examine closely their relationship with Him. They should be mindful that He is always willing to forgive, restore and renew those who come humbly and honestly to Him.

The resurrection: a very special day to remember

Great blessings from keeping the Lord's Day

Spurgeon's beggar—and the beautiful bride

Charles Haddon Spurgeon told about a generous and compassionate rich man, who gave six coins to a poor and wretched beggar. The beggar responded by stealing the seventh coin. Spurgeon reminded his listeners that God had graciously given mankind six out of seven days to spend on our work and on legitimate interests and pleasures, but we have stolen the other day. God's holy Sabbath day is not remembered or observed by the world at large. Often it is also ignored or rejected by those claiming to know Him.

A Welsh pastor shared an incident with me about a wedding reception, which illustrated the same point. There is a danger in his illustration! We must never feel any pity whatsoever for God: it has to be the other way round. He is the almighty Sovereign and Creator and Sustainer of the universe, with limitless power and authority. That power raised Jesus Christ from the dead. Rather, the point of the illustration is that we too easily forget the One who should be centre-stage in our thinking on His special day.

The guests had enjoyed (or endured!) the wedding ceremony and had 'ooohed and aaahed' at the attractive young bride in her beautiful, flowing, white wedding dress. Then came the reception. Everyone filed past the bridal party and made their appropriate comments. Then the meal! Some time after that, the happy pair were due to exit to an undisclosed place for their honeymoon. By then the occasion was really 'swinging' and a great time was being had by all. Well, nearly all! The groom was fully absorbed in exchanging jokes with members of his golf club. The guests were mixing well with each other as the background chatter reached top volume. The four parents hibernated to quieter corners to chat with their contemporaries. Just one person was at last noticed to be on her own, looking sad and embarrassed. Yes, that's right! It was the bride. She had been forgotten at her own wedding reception. That seems unbelievable, but it happened. How very sad!

What a day to remember!

Now, I could never have imagined my wife allowing that to happen! Certainly one could criticise the bride for not being pro-active. But, the point is that, on her special day, her new husband should have looked after her and stuck to her like super-glue! And her friends should have made an extra effort to encourage her and engage her attention.

Today, Bible-believing Christians rightly talk much of the resurrection of their Lord. But why do we ignore His wishes—more than that, His command— about how we should treat Him on His weekly special day? I refer to the Lord's Day, the Christian Sabbath. It is a day when we should remember that God created the world in six days and rested on the seventh day, mankind's first full day. On that day we should reflect that He has redeemed us from bondage, as He did for His physical people, Israel. But it is even more special than that: it is an opportunity to remember that the Lord Jesus Christ rose from the dead, and that He is Lord of all. Many churches and thousands of Christians seem to think that their obligations are met simply by holding services. He is often side-lined for much of the rest of His holy day. That really is sad!

But what a day to remember! We recall an Olympic gold medalist's day of achievement long after the event. A piece of gold marks that, for someone who will lose in the future and who, like us, will soon pass from the arena of life. But God gives us His weekly Lord's Day to keep and enjoy as a 'resurrection Sunday' remembrance of Him. On that day we can be blessed and a blessing to others. We lose greatly by not doing that, and dishonour His name through our neglect or rebellion. But we must learn how to keep it to receive and pass on those blessings.

'Sabbatarians' are unpopular, but Sunday sportsmen are very popular!

Believers in the resurrection of Christ should have an Easter Sunday every week! At the start of the week, we should rejoice in Jesus' resurrection and all that it means to us. Yet 'Sabbatarians', the name sometimes scornfully applied to those who hold dear the Christian Sabbath, often get a bad press. We are depicted as legalistic stick-in-the-muds from a bygone age, theological dinosaurs and kill-joys! It seems that some Christians have greater respect for those engaging in Sunday sport than those who teach the duty and privilege of keeping the Lord's Day.

Eric Liddell and 'Chariots of Fire'

Some Christian sportsmen must think that Eric Liddell, popularised by the film 'Chariots of Fire', was going too far. He refused to compete in the final of the 100 metres at the Paris Olympic Games on the Lord's Day. 'Young person, stand for Sunday,' he said, 'for by losing it you will lose far more than the day: you will lose the spirit that it stands for'. The popular 'flying Scotsman', who also represented his country's rugby team on the left wing, lived out what he taught. He served the Lord unstintingly, until his death in a Japanese prisoner of war camp. Amazingly, after having decided not to run on Sunday, the way opened for him to run in the final of the 400 metres on the Monday, and he won it in new Olympic record time! But Liddell's lesson is not that we shall always be successful if we honour God and His day. Rather, we should follow his example of crucifying our preferences and ambitions and putting God first, even when it seems we must lose out. And we will never know if Eric Liddell would have beaten the other British 'flyer', Harold Abrahams, in that 100 metres final!

The successes of Bernhard Langer and Jonathan Edwards

Bernhard Langer's championship golf success on an Easter Sunday and Jonathan Edwards' gold medal in the first Olympics of the new millennium, were both loudly acclaimed. Both are Christians. Edwards is on record, before he changed his once clear stance on not competing on the Lord's Day, as saying: 'Sunday is the best day of the week for me. Foremost, for the chance to meet together with other Christians to worship God and also to rest from all the other things which make the rest of the week so hectic. I'm sure God doesn't institute rules without reasons and one day a week of rest is meant for our physical and spiritual well-being.' Did God change his 'reasons' about His 'rules'?

We must assess from the Bible how we should keep resurrection Sunday each week and keep consistent, rather than to follow blindly any successful Christian sportsman.

Sir Jack Hobbs

Consider the position of, arguably, English cricket's greatest ever opening batsman, Sir Jack Hobbs. He was to English cricket what Babe Ruth was to US baseball. (I say 'arguably'—I have to vote for a fellow Yorkshireman, Sir Len Hutton, as cricket's best opener!) An attitude like Hobbs' is indeed rare in these days of whole-scale Sunday sport. One wonders if he could continue to play, were he alive today. He said 'I do not think I should [play cricket on Sunday], because one day's rest is essential' and added that he did 'not wish to do anything that would injure the cause of Christianity. I cannot act contrary to my principles.' There is a formidable list of committed Christians to whom the Lord's commandment and approval meant more than winning a medal or achieving excellence. Mark Roberts' compilation headed 'The Lord's Day: 100 Leaders Speak Out' (published by LDOS) is most helpful here. He cites twelve

Christian sports stars, and many more leaders on the world stage, who refused to conform to the world's failure to remember the Sabbath.

Jovial Johnny Lawrence

One of the sportsmen is jovial Johnny Lawrence, an all-rounder and (another!) Yorkshireman who played for Somerset County Cricket Club. He was my coach long before I came to know the risen Lord. His bright and genial character and sense of fun made him a wonderful advertisement for the Lord's Day he loved and the Lord who gave him that day. Johnny loved his cricket, but He loved His Lord and His special day better.

Mick Jones, New Zealand Rugby Union's 'destroyer'

Mick Jones, the powerful All Blacks rugby back row 'destroyer', is another. He refused to play on the Lord's Day against Wales in a Rugby World Cup semi-final. He stated 'I certainly feel happier adhering to my principles and standards of not playing on a Sunday. It would be hypocritical to change now just because there is a World Cup semi-final coming up. I would love to play, in terms of the opportunity, but I put God first.' On an international flight, seated next to a senior Rugby Union official, my opportunity to share Christ was greatly enhanced because of the respect he had for Jones, both as a world-class loose forward, and as a man of integrity and principle.

Barrington Williams, Olympic athlete

Another Olympic jumper and sprinter, Barrington Williams, said: 'I made a promise to the Lord that I will not take part in sports events on Sundays. Even if it is at the very top, I will jump on Saturday night and Monday morning, but not on Sundays. If it comes down to it, God comes first, athletics second. Sunday is God's day.' His baggage at the Olympics Village is said to have included a good supply of Christian literature to help him to share his faith with other athletes. He had his priorities right in that, too! His reward will be greater than any Olympic medal!

Euan Murray and the Rugby World Cup 2011: 'It's basically all or nothing, following Jesus.'

Euan Murray once was been Scotland's regular first choice as a prop forward. For the uninitiated, that means he was one of the big, strong, front row men in the scrum, arguably the toughest and most combative place to be on a rugby field. The Scottish coach described him as 'the best scrummager.' It was only about three years before the 2011 World Cup Competition in New Zealand that Murray decided not to play rugby on the Lord's day. That decision could not have been lightly taken for a well-established international player, whose whole career could easily have been jeopardised. Christian standards have been seriously eroded in a relatively short time-span. Now many Christians happily seek to justify playing and watching sport on the day to be set aside for God's worship and service. Some would now criticise Murray for his brave stance. One wonders if a 21st Century Eric Liddell would be acclaimed by Christian churches now, if he refused to run in a 100 metres Olympic final, held on a Sunday?

Below, in italics, is a verbatim copy of one report about Murray on the world wide web.

Devout Christian Euan Murray has questioned the need for Rugby World Cup matches to be played on Sundays.

The Glasgow-born prop, 31, has chosen to prioritise his faith this weekend, meaning he will miss Scotland's Pool B clash with Argentina on Sunday.

"I don't see why there have to be games on Sundays," said Murray. "I hope things will change in future."

Geoff Cross will replace Murray, who has been dubbed by Scotland coach Andy Robinson as "the best scrummager".

Murray will hope that he has done enough in previous matches to get his place in the team back for next week's match against England, which takes place on a Saturday.

Back in 2008, Murray did play on a Sunday when Scotland took on France in the Six Nations.

But, after his faith deepened, he announced a year later that he would no longer be available for selection on Sundays. At the time he said:

"It's basically all or nothing, following Jesus. I don't believe in pick 'n' mix Christianity. I believe the Bible is the word of God, so who am I to ignore something from it? I might as well tear out that page then keep tearing out pages as and when it suits me. If I started out like that there would soon be nothing left. I want to live my life believing and doing the things (God) wants and the Sabbath day is a full day. It's not a case of a couple of hours in church then playing rugby or going down the pub, it's the full day."

Murray is not the first sportsman to pull out of events because of his faith, one of the best-known being Eric Liddell who felt compelled to pull out of the heats for the 100m at the 1924 Olympics.

After finding out the schedule well in advance he decided to practise doing the 400m and subsequently won the gold medal, breaking both the Olympic and World records. More recently, triple jumper Jonathan Edwards missed the 1991 World Championships. After much deliberation he changed his mind two years later, just in time for qualifying, and went on to win bronze.

Should Scotland finish as runners-up in pool B, Murray would also miss the quarter-final and then possibly the semi-final, a similar situation to the one New Zealand star Michael Jones found himself in back in 1987 and 1991. He [Jones] was eventually omitted from the 1995 squad because he would have missed both the last-eight and last-four matches.

Game, set and match

You can see from Liddell, Lawrence, Jones, Williams and Murray that keeping the Lord's Day reflected faithfulness to principle, not a negative mind-set. Attractive personal preferences were secondary. Certainly, in the words of Sir Jack Hobbs, they would not 'do anything that would injure the cause of Christianity'. How much has that greatest cause of all been injured by an apparent ignorance or neglect of the Lord's Day on both sides of the Channel and the Atlantic by Christians? In England the flood-gates of Christian Sunday sports opened when a Christian won the first Wimbledon tennis final to be played on the Lord's Day, after rain had ruled out the final on Saturday. What an opportunity to declare that the prize of the resurrection Sabbath meant more than a mere trophy at Wimbledon! That would have been 'game, set and match' for the Lord's Day and the cause of our resurrected Saviour.

The unopened gift

Regretfully, the modern world has so influenced our ever-compromised churches that many Christians consider keeping the Lord's Day neither as a serious option, nor as a command to be obeyed. Some churches fail to teach why the Lord's Day is to be remembered as the Christian Sabbath. They press neither the great blessings, nor the grave damage, that flow from our response to God's command to 'Remember the Sabbath day, to keep it holy.' The Lord's Day must be the most sealed package in the unopened gift of resurrection benefits. Although some would seek to justify sincerely (or rationalise conveniently?) their position theologically, many just do not want to know. Perhaps they cling to their preferred lifestyle, even though keeping the Lord's Day could usher in a revived and vibrant spiritual life.

The scope of this chapter

This chapter does not present detailed theological argument to support the teaching and practice, once generally acknowledged but now sadly much eroded, that all the Ten Commandments, including the fourth, are binding on us today. However, this chapter does include paragraphs on 'The connection between the resurrection of Jesus and the Lord's Day' and 'The first-day-of-the-week resurrection Sabbath continued' as those subjects relate directly to the subject matter of this book, namely the resurrection of the Lord Jesus Christ.

For those who wish to explore in more detail the Biblical and theological support for the existence and continuation of the Lord's Day as the Christian Sabbath on the first day of the week, please turn to *Appendix One: The Lord's Day: the Christian's resurrection Sabbath remembrance*, where I have recommended a few publications, and outlined the Biblical position to encourage further study. For a brief response to those who say that the fourth commandment does not bind the Christian today, please see *Appendix Two: Ten Commandments— or only nine?*

The Ten Commandments are now our immediate subject, before looking at how Christ's resurrection impacts on the Lord's Day. We will then focus on the blessings which can be ours, and how we can appropriate them by honouring God in this important area of general neglect.

The Ten Commandments—'our tutor to bring us to Christ'

The Ten Commandments are also referred to as the 'Decalogue', the 'law', and God's 'moral law'. We could never be justified before God by keeping the moral requirements of His Ten Commandments. Even if that were theoretically possible, we would never achieve it. We have already broken His law and are guilty. 1 John 3, verse 4, tells us 'Whoever commits sin also commits lawlessness, and *sin is lawlessness*'. (My emphasis) Lawlessness implies a breaking and disregard for the law of God. But the moral law of God, summarised in those Ten Commandments, is according to Galatians 3 verse 24, 'our tutor to bring us to Christ'. Our very breaking of it shows us our need for mercy and forgiveness. The Holy Spirit uses the law to convict our hearts of our guilt and shame. It is that conviction that drives an unsaved sinner to seek God's pardon, in Jesus Christ alone and by faith alone in His redeeming sacrifice.

God works the same way on the hearts of erring believers to bring them to repentance, forgiveness, restoration of fellowship and spiritual renewal. A truly born again Christian cannot easily settle for a life of lawlessness. As John McArthur's Study Bible says, 'The first reason why Christians cannot practice sin is because sin is incompatible with the law of God which they love.'

John Bunyan—saved after being convicted of Sabbath breaking!

Men and women have come to Christ after being convicted by the Holy Spirit of the sin of Sabbath breaking. John Bunyan, the author of the world's second best seller, 'Pilgrim's Progress', describes in another book, 'Grace abounding to the chief of sinners', how that was true for him. He writes 'at that time I felt what guilt was, though never before, that I can remember'. Having stifled his conscience he nevertheless played, on the Sabbath, the then fashionable game of 'cat', when 'a voice did suddenly dart from heaven to my soul, which said "Wilt thou leave thy sins and go to heaven, or have thy sins and go to hell?" At this I was put to an exceeding maze; whereupon leaving my cat upon the ground, I looked up to heaven, and was as if I had, with the eyes of my understanding, seen the Lord Jesus looking down upon me, as being very hotly displeased with me, and as if He did severely threaten me with some grievous punishment for these and other my ungodly practices'. The great conviction of sin, underlined by his breaking the fourth commandment, led him to seek God's forgiveness and salvation. Those who would dispense with or ignore the Sabbath take away a means by which God can convict a sinner of his guilt, so vital before real personal conversion.

Preachers reading this will be encouraged to know that Bunyan's experience on that Lord's Day followed a morning sermon on Sabbath breaking by Rev. Christopher Hall, at the Church of England in Elstow. Bunyan had recovered from his initial troubled conscience by eating a good Sunday lunch, prepared by his wife. But when he went to play cat, God pursued him! How much we owe to that sermon, we may never know.

I myself was greatly helped, in the rebuilding of my Christian life after a time of rebellion and backsliding, by submitting on the question of keeping the Lord's Day. For me, it meant the end of high hopes in professional cricket, but it also meant a deeper knowledge of God that I had not experienced before. Those who undervalue the Sabbath also take away the key of blessing from other Christians who need to benefit from every means of grace available.

The Ten Commandments—a cavalier approach?

If we have really come to Christ, we will seek to please Him by keeping His commandments. That is the test of our love for Him and therefore of our conversion. Jesus said 'If you love Me, keep My commandments'.[127] Because Jesus is the eternal God, 'My commandments', which the Christian must 'keep' include the divinely given moral commands of both the Old and New Testaments. God's word is a complete entity. A careless or cavalier approach to obeying what God has said is not convincing evidence of having passed from death to life! Having said that, I appreciate the difficulties for many young (and older!) Christians today. The absence, or generally low standard of teaching about the Lord's Day and the example often given by church leaders and close friends at church, often give no help or godly example. Some teach or imply that it is too extreme, or even 'legalistic', to obey Jesus in the fourth command, to remember the Sabbath.[128] They expect detailed obedience in keeping the fifth, to honour our parents,[129] or the seventh, not to commit adultery.[130] Remembering the Sabbath is one of the first four of the Ten Commandments. Those four deal with man's relationship towards God. The next six concern direct conduct towards man. Jesus summarised the Decalogue as loving God first (commands one to four) and your neighbour second (commands five to ten).[131] Surely keeping the first four are the important basis for keeping the other six.

Special position of the Decalogue

The Decalogue is essentially moral in character and applies to all people, everywhere, for all time. The Ten Commandments are therefore different from God's ceremonial and health laws, both of which had 'sell by dates'. They are also far greater than Israel's national civil and criminal laws, which applied to them as a political entity, much as the laws of any country or state applies to its citizens today. Of course, the moral principles of the Ten Commandments are reflected in those laws.

The Decalogue describes God's changeless character.[132] The Ten Commandments were the only laws spoken in the hearing of the people,[133] written by God's own finger on tablets of stone,[134] and kept inside the ark of the covenant with the golden pot of manna and Aaron's rod that budded,[135] so they were very special commandments. They are specifically referred to in the Bible as the '*Ten* Commandments.'[136] The fourth command, to remember the Sabbath Day, has more space given to it than any other command. It bears repetition that it is binding today, and is to be obeyed. Clearly Jesus revered and observed it, as you would expect from the One who had come to fulfil the law, rather than destroy it.[137]

Legalistic or law-abiding?

We must not confuse 'legalism' with being 'law abiding'. Legalism imposes a set of secondary man-made laws and practices on already failing sinners. We are not to jump through other people's hoops. That is wrong, and can never bring spiritual blessing or knowledge of God. Being law-abiding is different. It can be spelled '*O-B-E-Y*'. It simply says 'I want to do what God says is right to do' and seeks to apply, faithfully and practically, the principles involved in the law to be obeyed. This is as true of not blaspheming and not worshipping idols as it is of keeping the Lord's Day.

Follow the law—it's a friend if you know God

One last illustration about our relationship to the law of God: when I lived in Belgium, I needed to find a factory in the Flemish countryside and I became hopelessly lost. I stopped at the road-side to enlist the help of a 'motard' (a black-leather clad policeman on a motor bike, complete with revolver). If I had seen that man in my rear view mirror my foot would have gone automatically for the brake. The law behind you makes you jumpy: we feel guilty on principle!

But this officer, though hard on the exterior, was very kind and helpful. He told me to follow him, and I did. My speed was considerably higher than if he had appeared behind me! I followed him through at least one red light! (Here my illustration breaks down.) But I was safe because I was following him. And he led me to where I wanted to be. It was the only time in Belgium that I took down the details of a policeman and reported him to the police! This time it was to commend him for his help.

When I follow God's moral law because I know and love Christ, God prepares my way and leads me safely to where I should be spiritually. The law is the friend, and not the foe, of a born again Christian! Follow it confidently by God's grace.

The connection between the resurrection of Jesus and the Lord's Day

The change of the Sabbath day of worship to the day of resurrection was anticipated in Psalm 118. Verses 22 to 24 of that Psalm state:

22 The stone which the builders rejected Has become the chief cornerstone.
23 This was the LORD's doing; It is marvellous in our eyes.
24 This is the day the LORD has made; We will rejoice and be glad in it.

That Psalm is applied to Jesus in the New Testament as the "stone which the builders rejected" who became the "chief cornerstone" (verse 22). See, for example, Ephesians 2 verse 20 and 1 Peter 2 verses 4 to 8. Also, Acts 4 verses 10 to 12 is especially relevant, since it is quoted in the context of the resurrection of the Lord Jesus Christ. Those verses state:

10 Let it be known to you all, and to all the people of Israel, that by the name of Jesus Christ of Nazareth, whom you crucified, whom God raised from the dead, by Him this man stands here before you whole.
11 This is the 'stone which was rejected by you builders, which has become the chief cornerstone.'
12 Nor is there salvation in any other, for there is no other name under heaven given among men by which we must be saved.

The Psalm prophetically teaches that Jesus' becoming the 'chief cornerstone' 'was the LORD's doing' and was 'marvellous' in their eyes. Equally prophetically in verse 24 we read '*This is the day* which the LORD has made; we will rejoice and be glad in it'. Which 'day' was meant? The crowning achievement of the Lord Jesus was His glorious resurrection from the dead, which made the 'rejected stone' of Calvary's cross the risen 'chief cornerstone'. So it was that day of resurrection which was prophetically emphasised in Psalm 118 as 'the day' in which 'we will rejoice and be glad'. The Lord's Day was resurrection day, and the principle of keeping one day in seven had found its fulfillment in the Person and work of the Lord Jesus.

The first-day-of-the-week resurrection Sabbath continued

Initially, the Jews carried on remembering the seventh day, even after the resurrection of Jesus. The initial co-existence of the two (first and seventh day) Sabbaths, leading to the gradual change to the first day Sabbath only, had the full approval of the apostles and the early church. The apostles adopted the first-day Sabbath: Paul preached to the assembled disciples at Troas on the first day of the week 'when the disciples came together to break bread'. He told the Corinthian church not to have a collection when he came to their customary meeting on the first day of the week, but to store their gifts instead. Even in exile on the Isle of Patmos, the 'Lord's Day' was remembered by the apostle John. That continued whilst the seventh-day Jewish Sabbath crumbled and disappeared, without unnecessary dispute. The Lord's Day maintained the principle of six days' activity followed by the Sabbath after those six days. (Acts 20 verses 6–7; 1 Corinthians 16 verses 1–2; Revelation 1 verse 10.)

The change of Sabbath from the seventh day to the first day is a tremendous evidence for the historicity of the resurrection of the Lord Jesus. For converted orthodox Jews to change their Sabbath, something extraordinary was needed! That was the case: Jesus had conquered the tomb!

In AD 70 history stepped in to complete the transformation from seventh day to first day Sabbath. Jerusalem was destroyed and the Jewish order of things evaporated. There was no nation of Israel, no priesthood, no sacrificial system or Temple worship, and no seventh-day Sabbath. But the Lord's Day continued as a testimony to God's unchanging moral law and to the glorious resurrection of the Lord Jesus Christ. It continues as that reminder today!

So how can I be blessed by keeping 'Easter Sunday' each week?

That is really the wrong question! When God tells us to obey Him we should do it anyhow, even if we can only expect that personal hardship and inconvenience will follow. It is more important to honour Him than to seek even 'spiritual blessing' for myself. However, we do know that God honours those who honour Him,[138] and we are always spiritually blessed when we trust and obey Him.

The blessing God promises to those who keep His day are summarised in Isaiah 58, verses 13 and 14, which are reproduced in the next paragraph. The God-given conditions for being blessed are clearly expressed there, and have to be read with the other conditions detailed in Exodus 20 verses 8 to 11. We will look at that scenario now and the wonderful help that God gives to individuals and churches who have adopted keeping the Lord's Day as a weekly life-style. We will then look at how Jesus spent His Sabbaths. May God guide us into a deeper and richer experience of our risen Lord, as we make each Lord's Day a weekly 'Easter Sunday' Sabbath.

Let us first consider the principles enunciated in Exodus 20 and in Isaiah 58.

What does the Bible say?

We will start by quoting the two passages in full. It is always good to start with the word of God! Exodus 20 verses 8 to 11 tells us:

8 Remember the Sabbath day, to keep it holy.

9 Six days you shall labour and do all your work,

10 but the seventh day is the Sabbath of the LORD your God. In it you shall do no work: you, nor your son, nor your daughter, nor your male servant, nor your female servant, nor your cattle, nor your stranger who is within your gates.

11 For in six days the LORD made the heavens and the earth, the sea, and all that is in them, and rested the seventh day. Therefore the LORD blessed the Sabbath day and hallowed it.

Isaiah 58 verses 13 and 14 states:

13 If you turn away your foot from the Sabbath, From doing your pleasure on My holy day, And call the Sabbath a delight, The holy day of the LORD honourable, And shall honour Him, not doing your own ways, Nor finding your own pleasure, Nor speaking your own words,

14 Then you shall delight yourself in the LORD; And I will cause you to ride on the high hills of the earth, And feed you with the heritage of Jacob your father. The mouth of the LORD has spoken.

It leads on to these verses in the next chapter, Isaiah 59:

1 Behold, the LORD's hand is not shortened, That it cannot save; Nor His ear heavy, That it cannot hear.

2 But your iniquities have separated you from your God; And your sins have hidden His face from you, So that He will not hear.

The blessings promised

These key passages confirm that God requires Sabbath observance within the moral law of His Ten Commandments. They show the principles upon which He works to bless us. But first, consider the great spiritual advantages that He graciously gives to those who honour Him on His special day.

1. A rest from everyday work is given to us.

2. We can help others also to be blessed, by promoting a rest from everyday work.

3. We are reminded each week of what holiness is in practice. That helps us during the week.

4. The Sabbath becomes a 'delight' to us, not drudgery, as we obey from the heart.

5. God is honoured, with all that springs from that.

6. As a result of keeping His day, we find our 'delight' in the LORD Himself, in all our days.

7. We are lifted up by Him to heights otherwise unattainable.

8. God will feed us with His heritage of promises. Like Jacob we fail, but God is faithful to us.

9. We receive assurance from His word.

10. We will see God's salvation and His answers to prayer, when we repent and keep His day.

'A fatal condition'

That list of promised blessings is comprehensive and amazing. Little wonder that Satan uses worldly counter-attractions to dull the spiritual awareness of Christians. He resents the generous interest God gives us on our investment of one day in seven consecrated to Him. Should we, then, be surprised when an unsaved person, thus without spiritual understanding, is deceived into thinking that keeping the fourth command is less important than his Sunday free time, sports, television, amusements and leisure activities?

Under the title 'A fatal condition' a recent edition of DayOne Magazine revealed:

Morbus Sabbaticus is a peculiar disease.

1. The symptoms vary but never interfere with the appetite.

2. It never lasts more than 24 hours.

3. No physician is ever called.

4. It is contagious.

The attack comes on suddenly on Sunday. No symptoms are ever felt on Saturday night. The patient awakes as usual, feeling fine and eats a hearty breakfast. Shortly thereafter the attack strikes and lasts till noon; then the patient is much improved and able to take a ride, visit friends, take a nap, or read a Sunday paper. The patient eats a hearty snack but the attack comes on again and lasts through the early evening. Patient is able to go to work on Monday as usual. The ailment is often fatal to the soul.

Which of us have not seen those symptoms at work, and but for God's grace might still be suffering from them ourselves now? Perhaps they still linger for some.

But what a return on investment!

It is a true but sad comment that many Christians, on both sides of the Atlantic Ocean and the English Channel, seem to follow the Sunday example of those on the broad way that leads to destruction rather than to deny themselves, take up their cross and follow their risen Lord. He said that it is only the narrow way that leads to life[139],[140] We all need reminding that just as resurrection followed crucifixion, so our experience of the risen Christ follows living a death-to-self life. Although the narrow way has no attraction to those who prefer the lifestyle of the broad way, we walk it with the Lord of the empty tomb. In step with Him on that living way, He gives us His daily peace, joy, strength and purpose. God adds a huge return on the capital investment in His Sabbath: rest, blessing to others, desire for holiness, delightful Sundays, God being honoured, God Himself becoming our delight, spiritual uplift, spiritual food, assurance, God's saving grace and answered prayer! How foolish to miss all that through failure to meet the conditions that He, in His wisdom, imposes upon us for our good.

What, then, are His conditions?

Conditions for blessing

Look again at Isaiah 58 and 59 and Exodus 20. Remember that God always keeps His word. If you have come to Christ as your living Saviour, and fulfil His conditions of how you keep the weekly Sabbath remembrance of His great acts of creation, redemption and resurrection, the blessings already discussed above *will be yours*. Of that, there can be absolutely no doubt. God's honour depends upon it, and many have proved that, as always, He is as good as His word.

Here are His conditions:

1. *Remember* His day. To forget it, neglect it, reduce it or reject it is sin in itself, and will also preclude you from His added 'fringe' blessings you could have acquired in keeping it.

2. Make *holiness* your goal. Holy things were things 'set apart' for God. See in how many ways you can set the Sabbath aside positively for Him.

3. *Resist* any temptation to do your *normal weekly work* on Sunday, unless it comes under one of the exceptions permitted by Jesus in cases of emergency, necessity, food preparation, compassion, helping the needy or sick, or gospel presentation.

4. Be *responsible for others* under your roof or your influence and do not be ashamed to insist that they do not break the fourth commandment whilst under

your care or influence. Lose popularity rather than deny the principle—God will honour you!

5. *Avoid* not only weekday work, but also seeking *your own pleasure* (as opposed to finding God's pleasure in seeking to put Him first). Your favourite activities are for another day.

6. Do *not* do '*your own ways*'. I am to do what God wants, not what I want. His word and His will are to be my pursuit, not my preferences or others' practices.

7. Make *your words count* for Him. Whereas no one should act in legalistic judgement of others, there are six days of the week when we can legitimately discuss our pleasures and concerns. A good aim for each Sunday service is to meet ready to share informally our morning quiet-time thoughts and to discuss constructively the messages preached or hymns sung.[141] My words can also count in comforting the sorrowing, encouraging the weak, rebuking the wayward, and welcoming the return of backsliders.

8. On His day, be involved in evangelism, knowing '*the Lord's hand is not shortened, That it cannot save*'. That may mean preaching, testifying, reading Scripture, singing or leading worship publicly. It may also mean inviting friends to church (and home for a meal, if appropriate), or looking around to welcome the lonely or those who are strangers. It may mean work in the hospitals or prisons, or visiting those in need

9. Be *prayerful*, knowing that '*His ear [is not] heavy, That it cannot hear*'. If we are honouring the Lord on His day, our attitude will be attuned to prayer, and we will find it natural to pray. We will pray individually and with others.

10. We need to *search* our *hearts* to make sure that there are no unforgiven '*iniquities [that] have separated [us] from [our] God*' and no unconfessed '*sins [that] have hidden His face from [us], So that He will not hear.*' We should always keep short accounts with God, and walk in the light with each other and with Him. We gratefully remember that 'the blood of Jesus Christ, His Son, cleanses us from all sin'. The Lord's Day should be a time when the living Lord's word, worship, and fellowship vibrate with such harmony in our spirits, that the discordant notes of sin and rebellion are easily detected by us. They should be silenced by prompt repentance and confession to Jesus.

The Master's example—how Jesus spent His Sabbaths

Mark chapter 1, verses 21 to 34, shows us how Jesus spent the Sabbath. He enthusiastically went about His worship on the Sabbath and 'immediately' entered the synagogue when he arrived at Capernaum. He taught God's word. He challenged people with the truth and authority of that word. He manifested and demonstrated God's sovereign delivering power. He went to the house of

His disciples. He healed a sick woman and dealt with the needs of the many sick and demon-possessed people.

In chapters 2 and 3 of the same gospel His pattern of observing the Sabbath continued. He walked with his disciples and there discussed spiritual and Biblical matters with them. He answered the questions of those who were hostile to Him and His message. He explained the reason for the Sabbath, His Lordship over it and what to do on it. Again, He went into the place of worship, the synagogue. He dealt with the spiritual and physical needs of many people and showed His love and power in so doing. The application is compelling. If the sinless Son of God saw the need and desirability to keep the Sabbath, then how much more do we need to keep it? We know that His keeping the day pleased the Father, because He declared Himself to be 'well pleased'[142] with His Son, and Jesus said that He always did the Father's will.[143]

And you?

You either have tried to obey Christ and keep His day, with God's help, or you have been ignorant, neglectful, incomplete, or rebellious about it. If the latter, will you now confess any Sabbath-breaking along with other sins and seek His forgiveness and blessing as you give the Lord of the empty tomb your Sundays? The detail of how you keep them is something you work out with God, based on the principles of His word. Two equally committed Christians may differ on some aspects of how they work out the principle of remembering the Sabbath. That is not a problem as long as each submits to the Sovereignty of the risen Lord. If so, they will be prepared to examine their motives and practices openly before God, and seek His help to change where necessary. They will search God's word for principles, commands and examples to follow.

But a superficial search for unanimity of detail *would be* legalism. Rather, we should turn back to loving Christ in the keeping of His commandments, including number four. If God has our hearts and willingness on that point, He will be honoured and we will be blessed.

Of course, some have not kept the Lord's Day because they do not belong to the Lord yet. You cannot keep the Lord's Day unless you know the Lord of the Day! If you do not know Him, your urgent priority and need is to call on Him to save you. When you do that, start your Christian life with the determination to walk closely with Him each day and each week. That will include building a daily quiet time of reading the Bible and praying. You will need to be disciplined in attending Christian fellowship meetings and seeking to make keen Christian friends. It will also involve your weekly keeping of the Sabbath, with all its spin-off benefits. The Lord's Day will be a wonderful help to your going on with the risen Christ.

The Lord's Day: the Christian's resurrection Sabbath remembrance

1. Further reading

Those who want to study the Biblical position for the Lord's Day, our Sunday, as the Christian first-day of the week Sabbath would profit from consulting the following publications, available from the publishers of this book, unless another publisher is indicated:

Bishop Daniel Wilson's classic *The Lord's Day*
Bishop J.C. Ryle's *A Day to Keep* (being an excerpt from his *Knots Untied*)
J P Thackray's two booklets *The Lord's Day principles and practice* and *The Lord's Day—'Special or Sabbath?'*
Dr Joseph A Pipa's *The Lord's Day* (Christian Focus)
Walter Chantry's *Call the Sabbath a Delight* (Banner of Truth)
Nelson McCausland's broadsheet *The Sunday Question*
John Roberts' booklet *The Lord's Day: A positive approach.*

They show that the continuation of the pre-legal principle of specifically keeping one day in seven is, very happily, still binding on us today. It is a bond of blessing. The first day of the week (our Sunday) has God's authority and sanction for becoming that Sabbath, which we know as 'the Lord's Day'.

2. A brief outline of the position

1. 'Sabbath' means 'rest' or 'cessation'. God made the Sabbath before He decreed the moral law of the Ten Commandments. Initially, the Sabbath was one day's rest after six days of creation.
Genesis 2 verses 2,3

2. Although the Sabbath was instituted before the Ten Commandments, the fourth command was to 'remember' it. Exodus 20 verses 8 to 11

3. Even if the fourth command had marked the creation of the Sabbath, we should nevertheless keep it as we are dealing with God's unchanging moral law.

4. Three principles applied to the Sabbath: first, no daily work; second, it had to be holy or 'set-apart', both from other days and from the way in which non-God fearing people would keep it; and third, those with authority were

responsible for those under their roof or influence. That day understandably became a day of worship and a cessation from the work and pursuits of the normal week.

Leviticus 23 verse 3

5. The Sabbath was also a remembrance of Israel's redemption from slavery in Egypt.

Deuteronomy 5 verses 12 to 15

(In those days, the timing of the original Sabbath had been lost in captivity, but the principle of one day in seven continued and the day of redemption marked the Sabbath's continuation.)

6. The principle of working six days and resting on the seventh was extended to the gathering of manna in the wilderness, though God did not say which was 'day seven' or 'day one'.

Exodus 16 verses 22 to 31

7. The Sabbath was proclaimed by the prophets as a source of blessing, if kept from the heart, and a cause of divine judgement, if broken. Isaiah, Jeremiah, and Ezekiel are examples of this fact. Proper worship of God in the Temple was tied to Sabbath obedience, and conversely the failure to keep the Sabbath coincided with idolatry.

Isaiah 56 verses 1 to 8; Isaiah 58 verses 13,14; Jeremiah 17 verses 19 to 27; Ezekiel 20 verses 10 to 32

8. In the rebuilding of Jerusalem, and the return to proper worship in the Temple, the people's attitude to the Sabbath was treated as fundamental. During the prophetic ministries of Ezra and Malachi, the revival under the leadership of Nehemiah included a vigorous enforcement of Sabbath observance, and removing even the opportunity for Sabbath trading. Nehemiah 13 verses 15 to 22; Nehemiah 10 verses 28 to 39, especially verse 31

9. The change of the Sabbath day of worship to the day of resurrection was anticipated in Psalm 118. Verses 22 to 24 of that Psalm state:

22 The stone which the builders rejected Has become the chief cornerstone.

23 This was the LORD's doing; It is marvellous in our eyes.

24 This is the day the LORD has made; We will rejoice and be glad in it.

That Psalm is applied to Jesus in the New Testament as the 'stone which the builders rejected' who became the 'chief cornerstone' (verse 22). See, for example, Ephesians 2 verse 20 and 1 Peter 2 verses 4 to 8. Also, Acts 4 verses 10 to 12 is especially relevant, since it is quoted in the context of the resurrection of the Lord Jesus Christ. Those verses state:

10 let it be known to you all, and to all the people of Israel, that by the name of Jesus Christ of Nazareth, whom you crucified, whom God raised from the dead, by Him this man stands here before you whole.

11 This is the stone which was rejected by you builders, which has become the chief cornerstone.'

12 Nor is there salvation in any other, for there is no other name under heaven given among men by which we must be saved.

The Psalm prophetically teaches that Jesus' becoming the 'chief cornerstone' 'was the LORD's doing' and was 'marvellous' in their eyes. Equally prophetically in verse 24 we read 'This is the day which the LORD has made; we will rejoice and be glad in it'. Which 'day' was meant? The crowning achievement of the Lord Jesus was His glorious resurrection from the dead, which made the 'rejected stone' of Calvary's cross the risen 'chief cornerstone'. So it was that day of resurrection which was prophetically emphasised in Psalm 118 as 'the day' in which 'we will rejoice and be glad'. The Lord's Day was resurrection day, and the principle of keeping one day in seven had found its fulfillment in the Person and work of the Lord Jesus.

(Little wonder that the day of Pentecost, when the Father sent the Spirit on the church had been planned by Him to mark this first day of the week also! The incarnate 'Lord of the Sabbath' chose the Lord's Day to bestow His Spirit on His Church.)

10. The New Testament teaches that the Sabbath continued after the Old Testament period. Jesus said it was made for man and He declared Himself on earth to be 'Lord of the Sabbath'. Jesus regarded the Sabbath as real as winter and told the Jerusalemites to pray that persecution would not force them to flee either in the winter or on a Sabbath.

Mark 2 verses 27, 28; Matthew 24 verse 20

11. The strict observance of the Sabbath in the New Testament era was such that no further command to keep it was needed in the New Testament, and the law upholding it was already known to be 'holy, and the commandment holy, and just and good'.

Romans 7 verse 12

12. Initially the Jews carried on remembering the seventh day, even after the resurrection of Jesus. The initial co-existence of the two (first and seventh day) Sabbaths, leading to the gradual change to the first day Sabbath only, had the full approval of the apostles and the early church. The apostles adopted the first-day Sabbath: Paul preached to the assembled disciples at Troas on the first day of the week 'when the disciples came together to break bread'. He told the Corinthian church not to have a collection when he came to their customary meeting on

the first day of the week, but to store their gifts instead. Even in exile on the Isle of Patmos, the 'Lord's Day' was remembered by the apostle John. That continued whilst the seventh-day Jewish Sabbath crumbled and disappeared, without unnecessary dispute The Lord's Day maintained the principle of six days' activity followed by the Sabbath after those six days.

Acts 20 verses 6,7; 1 Corinthians 16 verses 1,2; Revelation 1 verse 10

13. The change of Sabbath from seventh day to first is a tremendous evidence for the historicity of the resurrection of the Lord Jesus. For converted orthodox Jews to change their Sabbath, something extraordinary was needed! That was the case: Jesus had conquered the tomb!

14. In AD 70 history stepped in to complete the transformation from seventh day to first day Sabbath. Jerusalem was destroyed and the Jewish order of things evaporated. There was no nation of Israel, no priesthood, no sacrificial system or Temple worship, and no seventh day Sabbath. But the Lord's Day continued as a testimony to God's unchanging moral law and to the glorious resurrection of the Lord Jesus Christ. It continues as that reminder today!

15. God has always made allowances to do work or activity in case of emergencies or necessities, knowing that He sees and knows our hearts and true motives. For example, in Matthew 12, Jesus sanctioned eating food, the work of caring for those who are ill, showing compassion, travelling for worship and fellowship, and meeting unforeseen emergencies. This is all consistent, of course, with Isaiah 58 where God encourages the proclamation of His message, announcing liberty to captives and doing good to others who are in need.

Matthew 12 verses 1 to 22; Isaiah 58

16. The divinely appointed weekly Lord's Day Sabbath, is commanded by the fourth of God's changeless moral commandments, and must not be confused with the extra sabbaths of ceremony or tradition that legalisers tried to foist upon the consciences of the early Christians at Colosse. (Colossians 2 verses 14 to 17). These extra requirements, which included certain 'holy days' or 'new moons', could not save or bless anyone. (See Galatians 4 verses 10–11). These legalistic additives are referred to as part of the 'handwriting of requirements' which were nailed to Christ's cross. They are extinguished debts, paid off in full and now null and void, which therefore have no hold or claim on us today. They are shadows instantly dispelled by resurrection life and light. They are irrelevant. As Joseph Pipa points out in *The Lord's Day* they were signs that pointed to Christ and are no longer needed. Thus we are to require no one to keep any of these. We seek to know the power of the risen Lord in our lives, not adherence to unnecessary requirements of past observance. So today, if anyone wants to invest more time in worship and hearing the word of God on Good Friday or Christmas Day, well and good. But that is neither a necessary requirement for the investor, nor for

anyone else. And any such additional 'voluntary' investment of his time does not compare with God's command to keep His fourth commandment. But, as Pipa points out, the same arguments apply to a legalistic insistence on keeping a *seventh day* Sabbath. That has gone because God has ushered in the Lord's Day Sabbath on the first day of the week to commemorate resurrection. That seventh day observance has been fulfilled in the first day, Lord's Day. Neither the Colossians nor we should judge any who do not keep the seventh day any longer. This truth not only deals with the error of Seventh Day Adventism, but also challenges any Christian who wrongly seeks to avoid practising the Decalogue's timeless principle of keeping one day in seven holy. The fact that the old seventh day Sabbath has gone, does not mean that God does not require us to keep one day in seven for Him. The Christian must do this out of obedience for the Lord he loves on the day of resurrection, the Lord's Day.

Ten Commandments— or only nine?'

Some argue that the fourth commandment does not apply to Gentiles today but only to Jews. However, this creates a number of problems, which are very hard to answer, in context, from the Bible. In considering this question, the ten points below should be borne in mind.

1. The phrase 'the law' is synonymous with the Ten Commandments and is an amplification of Christ's twin requirement in Mark 12, verse 29, that 'you shall love the LORD your God with all your heart, with all your soul, with all your mind, and with all your strength' and that 'You shall love your neighbour as yourself.' Further, the New Testament variously states that the guilt, produced by the effect of the law on the heart, belongs to man generally and not uniquely to the Jew.

2. Romans 2, verse 15, teaches that Gentiles show that the work of the law is written in the heart of man. The whole world is guilty, but where there is no law there is no transgression. This confirms that the law is worked into man's being by God. When God's finger wrote His law upon stone, He simply reminded men of sin's defilement as part of the fall.

3. In Romans 6, verse 18, a Gentile church is told it has been freed from the law by the death and resurrection of Christ. But you cannot be freed from what never bound you! And a Gentile church is not Jewish! The same thought occurs in Galatians, 5 verse 1, and in the same letter, chapter 3 verses 23 and 24, the non-Jewish Christians were told that they had been 'kept under guard by the law' and that the law was their tutor (and Paul's also) to 'bring them to Christ.' So we logically deduce that the law also applied to the Galatian believers, who were not a Jewish part of the church.

4. Some argue that the fourth commandment is there to teach the Gentiles that God had a special covenant with the Jews, but surely that reason is as ingenious as it is without warrant from Scripture. It is nowhere argued thus in the Bible. The Jews were simply given a privileged reminder of mankind's obligation under the whole law to remember that God was their Creator, by ceasing from work and by particularly devoting the day to resting in God in worship on that Sabbath day. It seems strange that some who argue, quite rightly, that the law still does exist and needs to be preached for God the Holy Spirit to convict of sin, can maintain that only nine commandments are applicable. This includes some dear and spiritual men of God, and one can only wonder

if culture and Christian peer pressure has had a far deeper effect on them than they have so far realised. That is a warning for us all. It seems that the support for this is from a weak argument from Colossians chapter 2 verse 16. Some who make the argument admit that, in the very same passage, the context concerns ceremonial aspects of the Jewish law, which only shadowed and pointed to the Lord Jesus Christ. They would agree that such rules are useless, man- made, and only legalistic. But is the principle of the weekly Sabbath, commanded by God in the Ten Commandments, accurately described as 'useless, man-made, and only legalistic'? If we still need God's law today, and if God expressed it in the Ten Commandments, despite the 'fact' that only nine were needed for all except the Jews, did God make a mistake with His mathematics initially? Or should He have included the Sabbath elsewhere? Or did He change His mind later? His own finger wrote 'Ten Commandments' in stone, not nine. 'What God has joined together, let not man separate' (Matthew 19 verse 6). The Colossians passage does not deal with the keeping of THE weekly creation Sabbath, now fulfilled in the resurrection Lord's Day, but with a legalistic insistence on keeping a spent seventh day or miscellaneous other days of no *current* importance. An interesting insight on all this came from a church leader who commented, "It is remarkable that Jesus should have spent so long in correcting the legalistic abuse of the Sabbath by the Pharisees, and demonstrated how it should be kept and remembered, if it was scrapped or about to be scrapped!" You do not overhaul a broken down car on the way to the scrap yard.

5. In Jeremiah 31 verses 31 to 34, referred to again in 32 verses 38 to 41,

and endorsing and enlarging on chapter 24 verse 7, the prophet predicts the work of regeneration in the heart of man under the new covenant by the presence of the Spirit of God. What is the product of the Holy Spirit? It is the writing of the law of God into the living, and newly willing, heart of man. This does not mean that the presence of God's law in his heart makes man a legalist! Rather, this demonstrates that the driving principle of all his obedience, (which is his conforming to the will of God), is a free and willing love for what God has revealed as His good and perfect will for man.

6. It is surprising that some churches, believers and respected Bible teachers have enthusiastically sought to distinguish between the other nine laws and the fourth commandment. The Roman Catholic Church also sought a reason to exclude and be free from a specific command, when it found it convenient to expel the command against idols and idolatry. As then with those desiring idolatry, so the result for those who would annul the command, to remember the Sabbath to keep it holy, is partial obedience. This is nothing less than disobedience. Some, who surprisingly hold this view, nevertheless have such a heart for the Lord and His word that, in practice, they live as if they did hold

to the Lord's Day Sabbath. But conduct follows Scripture, and this opens the way for others to feel free to honour God for only a fraction of the day, and worship communally only once, and/or work, and/or dine out, and/or travel to and from holidays, and/or participate in any sport, and/or attend a sporting event or match, and/or spend hours in entertainment and/or buy and sell. In other words, some seem to have a reason for wanting the Lord's Day to be just another day to leave them free for other things, and are grateful when spiritual men unwittingly give them that option. In practice it is, for them, only His day in token. Under this viewpoint it is man, not Christ, who decides what to do as 'the Lord of the Sabbath.'

7. The result is that Christ is given only some of the day. In the UK this has resulted in following the trend in spiritual dark and needy parts of Europe, or in parts of over-materialistic North America. The Lord's Day has thus been desecrated and God dishonoured. It has led to, in the European case, a sad but historical starvation of Bible teaching that has fathered a lack of spiritual appetite to feed at God's weekly Sabbath banquet. In the North American case a desire for materialistic ease and self-indulgent entertainment, has weakened and wounded the observance of the Lord's Day. In each case, consequently Sunday church attendance is often limited to once only—normally the morning worship—and then the day is viewed as free for an 'anything goes' afternoon and evening. How sad to be greatly blessed in large morning congregations in the USA, where initially one is encouraged to see a Biblical emphasis and an apparent spiritual hunger, and then return in the evening (if a meeting is still held in the evening) to numbers which make you think you have gate-crashed the choir practice or even the committee meeting. Even in the very large churches, where thousands still gather, the attendance rarely matches the normal morning congregation, especially when a major sporting fixture is in competition! Were those who did not come again more blessed by the Lord in their absence than they would have been by being present? What was the higher priority that kept them away? (Clearly some have legitimate duties that mean they cannot be there, such as mothers with babies and young children.)

8. Is not something wrong with the heart when there is reluctance to optimise the opportunities for worship, prayer, singing praises to Christ, hearing the reading of Scripture and serious ministry of Scripture, reading Christian books, informal fellowship, providing Christian hospitality, profitable spiritual time with the children and family, evangelism, visiting and so many activities which could bring down blessings? Do not the arguments for viewing the Lord's Day as any other day, result in a mere token-ism and prevent this day of resurrection from being a light in a dark place? The world may be expected to ignore God and

His commandments, and to justify their rebellious attitude and practices, when God's people fail to set them the proper example.

9. Removing the fourth commandment in its bearing upon the first day of the week seems to be for the purpose of freeing up the day *from* worship, rather than making it available *for* worship. The day should be freed from both legalistic distortion and from disobedient neglect of God's holy requirements, so that love for God can claim the whole day for freely given extended worship of Christ!

10. Practical spin-off from this is that young converts, or shallow Christians, will take their lead from the easiest option available. No wonder that many know more about Sunday TV soccer or the US televised ball game on the Lord's Day than about their Bibles. It is hardly surprising that they too come to regard leisure and entertainment as a more fluent topic of conversation than the morning message or the needs of missionaries. In both Europe and America, it is noticeable that the lack of loyalty to meeting in the evening of the Lord's Day spins over to mid-week meetings for essential prayer and Bible study.

1   Matthew 28 verses 11 to 15

2   1 Corinthians 5 verse 7; Exodus 12 verse 6

3   Matthew 28 verse 9, Luke 24 verse 38,39 and John 20 verse 27

4   Matthew 28 verse 17

5   Luke 23 verse 55

6   Dale Rhoton's 'The Logic of Faith' (STL), 'The Islam Debate' (Campus Crusade) for Christ published by (Here's Life Publishers Inc) by Josh McDowell and John Gilchrist investigate this more fully.

7   2 Timothy 3 verse 2

8   Matthew 1 verse 23

9   Romans chapter 6 explains its meaning since the resurrection.

10   John 2 verses 19, 21 to 22

11   Matthew chapter 12—especially verse 40

12   Also Matthew 20 verse 17 to 19. The Cross and the Resurrection were married together. They were a single continuous event in the Lord's teaching.

13   1 Corinthians 15

14   Check Acts 2 verses 24,32; 3 verses 15,26; 4 verse 10; 5 verse 30; 10 verse 40; 13 verses 30,33; and 17 verse 31.

15   1 Corinthians 15 verses 3,4

16   John 3 verse 16, Galatians 2 verse 20

17   1 Peter 2 verse 24

18   John 8 verse 58

19   John 14 verse 9 and 10 verse 30

20   Deuteronomy 6 verse 13 and 10 verse 20

21   Exodus 20 verse 3

22   Mark 2 verses 5 to 7

23   Dealt with in Chapter 2

24   To be understood as in the Great Commission, 'All authority is given unto me ...' Matthew 28 verses 18 to 20. The distinction in the phases of His humanity before and after the resurrection is often overlooked. No- one spits in His face now! He is the great and only Priest and King in heaven.

25   Isaiah 53 verses 4 to 6

26   1 Peter 2 verse 24

27   Luke 23 verse 44, John 19 verse 28, Matthew 27 verse 46, Matthew 27 verses 39 to 44

28   John 3 verse 36

29   John 19 verse 30

30   John 3 verse 36

31   1 John 1 verse 5 and Revelation 21 verse 23

32   2 Thessalonians 1 verse 9

33   Matthew 26 verses 6 to 13

34   Compare the punishment for sin described in Revelation 14 verses 10,11

35   John 14 verse 6 and Acts 4 verse 12

36   John 1 verse 14 and Luke 24 verse 19

37   John 5 verse 30

38   Romans 14 verses 10 to 12

39   1 John 2 verse 1

40   1 Corinthians 15 verse 56

41   Romans 14 verse 9

42   1 Thessalonians 4 verses 13 to 23

43   Ephesians 1 verse 6

44   Romans 8 verse 30

45   John 11 verse 25

46   Proverbs 18 verse 24

47   Philippians 1 verse 21 and 23, 2 Corinthians 5 verse 8

48   Hebrews 2 verse 14

49   Hebrews 13 verse 20

50   2 Corinthians 5 verse 17.

51   Hebrews 9 verse 27

52   Matthew 7 verse 7

53   1 Corinthians 15 verses 13, 14, 15, 17, 18 and 19

54   Galatians 2 verse 20

55   John 14 verse 6

56   John 1 verse 29

57   Ephesians 2 verse 8

58 Acts 16 verse 31

59 Acts 2 verse 21

60 John 1 verse 12

61 Romans 10 verses 9 and 10

62 Acts 4 verse 12

63 Colossians 1 verse 27

64 John 14 verse 23

65 Ephesians 3 verse 19

66 Luke 1 verse 47; Matthew 1 verse 23; Matthew 1 verse 21. The name Jehovah-is-Saviour is itself a further proof of the Deity of the Lord Jesus.

67 John 16 verse 7

68 Philippians 4 verse 13

69 Philippians 4 verse 7; Philippians 1 verse 21; Philippians 3 verse 10

70 Galatians 2 verse 20

71 2 Corinthians 13 verse 5

72 Acts 13 verses 50 to 52

73 1 Thessalonians 1 verses 9 and 10

74 Luke 10 verses 17 and 20

75 Hebrews 7 verse 25

76 John 14 verses 2 and 3

77 Revelation 5 verses 6 to 14

78 Revelation 2 verse 8

79 1 John 3 verse 2

80 1 Corinthians 15 verse 52

81 John 14 verse 6

82 2 Timothy 3 verse 16; 2 Timothy 2 verse 15

83 Colossians 1 verse 27

84 Acts 4 verse 12

85 Jonah 2 verse 9

86 Ephesians 2 verses 8,9; John 10 verse 28 and Philippians 4 verse 13

87 1 Timothy 1 verse 15

88 Hebrews 12 verse 2

89 John 20 verses 24 to 29

90 Matthew 7 verse 7

91 Mark 9 verse 24

92 Isaiah 53 verse 4

93 Philippians 4 verse 7

94 1 Peter 2 verse 24

95 Luke 18 verse 13

96 Romans 10 verse 13

97 Acts 4 verse 2

98 Galatians 2 verse 20

99 Romans 5 verse 1

100 1 Peter 1 verse 8

101 Jeremiah 29 verse 13

102 Matthew 7 verse 7

103 Romans 6 verse 11

104 Romans 6 verse 11

105 Romans 8 verse 34

106 1 John 3 verse 2

107 1 Corinthians 2 verse 2

108 Colossians 2 verse 6

109 Hebrews 12 verse 14

110 1 Thessalonians 5 verse 18

111 2 Thessalonians 3 verse 1

112 James 1 verse 5

113 James 3 verses 1 to 12

114 Proverbs 23 verse 26

115 Proverbs 4 verse 23

116 1 John 1 verse 7

117 James 4 verse 6

118 Psalm 12 verse 1

119 Psalm 12 verse 4

120 Isaiah 6 verse 5

121 John 14 verse 6

122 John 17 verse 17

123 John 16 verse 13

124 Revelation 21 verse 27

125 Galatians 2 verse 20

126 Proverbs 15 verse 3

127 John 14 verse 15

128 Exodus 20 verses 8 to 11

129 Exodus 20 verse 12

130 Exodus 20 verse 14

131 Matthew 22 verses 37 to 40

132 Malachi 3 verse 6

133   Deuteronomy 5 verse 2

134   Exodus 31 verse 18

135   Exodus 25 verse 16; Hebrews 9 verse 4

136   Exodus 34 verse 28

137   Matthew 5 verse 17

138   John 12 verse 26

139   Matthew 7 verses 13,14

140   Luke 14 verse 27

141   Hebrews 10 verse 25

142   Matthew 3 verse 17

143   John 8 verse 29

Also by Gerard Chrispin

Published by DayOne (dayone.co.uk)

How can ...?

How can God accept me?

ISBN 978–1–84625–654–7

How I can find God today

978–1–84625–656–4

How to become a real Christian

978–1–84625–656–1

Why God allows suffering

978–1–84625–667–7

These attractive yet frank, God centred, gospel presentations by Gerard Chrispin persuade each reader to examine his, or her, life afresh and to turn from sin to Jesus Christ. Each has 32 pages of quality photo illustrations, and they are good for different areas of Christian witness. Works focused on missions, church evangelism, open airs, visitation, youth, the student world, rest homes, hospitals and prisons have all benefited from them. Fitting easily into the pocket or handbag, they are ideal for giving to those we meet.

The Bible Panorama (3rd edition)

ISBN: 978-1-846252-07-5

672 PAGES

The Bible Panorama is a unique introduction to and survey of the Bible, giving an overview of each book of the Bible and taking into consideration the message of each verse, without actually being a verse-by-verse commentary.

It provides a series of very memorable outlines for each chapter of the Bible. It also includes a succinct but vigorous defence of the Bible, and concludes with a number of reading schemes to guide the reader through the Scriptures.

Many generations of devout readers of the Scriptures have found in them the words of eternal life. I commend this volume, whose purpose is to lead people of our day to a like precious faith, to all who are prepared to give the Bible an opportunity to speak to them.

LORD MACKAY OF CLASHFERN,
former Lord Chancellor of the United Kingdom

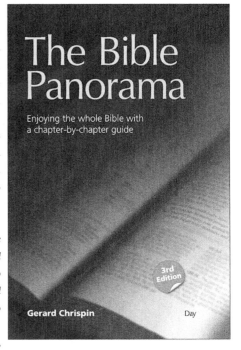

The Bible Panorama

Enjoying the whole Bible with a chapter-by-chapter guide

3rd Edition

Gerard Chrispin

Day

Mark Time!

ISBN: 978-1-84625-284-6

The stand-alone Mark Time book will repay careful reading. It gives a clear, no-nonsense explanation of the whole of Mark's Gospel, in 52 very short and easy-to-read chapters. Each chapter contains the whole text of Mark's Gospel on which it comments. The Bible versions, used in equal measure, are New International Version, New American Standard Bible, English Standard Version, and New King James Version.

Having said that the book is a 'stand-alone' title, the good news is that there are also two optional Mark Time correspondence courses which are simple without being simplistic, and which enable anyone following them to be sure that he or she has understood the text properly. You will find them enjoyable to use. Churches and groups find such correspondence courses extremely valuable both in reaching out with the gospel and in nurturing new Christians, or those needing a refresher course.

Mark Time is used for discussion groups by discussing the questions at the end of each chapter, as well as to encourage individuals throug the correspondence courses. It can be a real blessing, not only to individuals of various backgrounds and experience, but also to those working through Bible studies, Christian Unions, Youth Groups, Church and work-place fellowships, and in prisons.

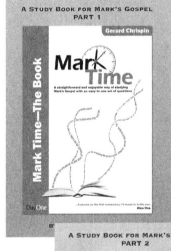

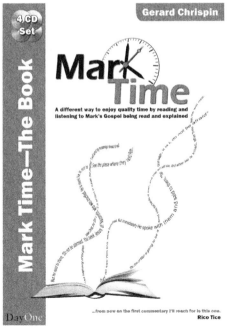

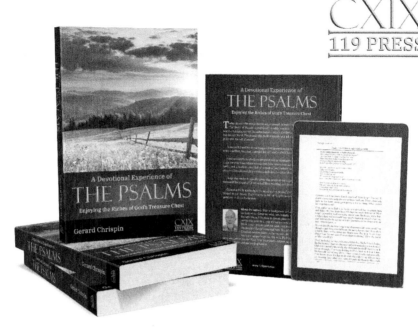

New book by Gerard Chrispin from 119Press through Amazon

Today all over the world people are confused, worried and—most of all—lost. The Book of Psalms shows God's readily available answer to each person, whether Christian or not, in each situation, who individually will trust God through His written Word. Please read this book regularly and ask God to speak to you and guide you. He will if you do!

. . . an accessible and heart-warming encouragement to the reader to place their trust in the crucified, risen and ascended Jesus Christ.—*Phil Chadder*

. . . a *treasure chest* from which we can pluck out spiritual gems to enrich our Christian life, a *war chest* from which we can withdraw reserves to aid us in our daily spiritual battle, and a *medicine chest* full of remedies with which we can treat our various ailments. I would heartily prescribe a daily dose!
—*Mike Mellor*

. . . helps the reader to quickly grasp the essential message of each Psalm, in the context of the gospel of Christ and of Him crucified and risen again.—*Steve Taylor*

. . . Gerard skilfully applies both the sharp sword of God's Word and the balm of the Gospel to our hearts. Each chapter is full of helpful insights as well as insightful questions.—*Jamie Southcombe*

A Devotional Experience of the Psalms: Enjoying the Riches of God's Treasure Chest
Gerard Chrispin | Large-Format, 404pp | Paperback and Hardcover Options